THE TATTOO

Photographic Credits

Christine Alicino - pages 259, 260, 263; Lance Barton - page 43; Bernice P Bishop Museum - page 56; Ph F Boizoi - page 42; Robert Butcher - page 212; Richard Campion - page 213; Stuart Davidson - cover, page 9; Sandi Fellman - pages 98, 105; Andreas Feininger - page 6; Myra Fourwinds - pages 46; Johnny's Photo Service - page 11; Shigeru Kuronuma - page 100; Philip Le Masurier - back cover, page 126; Don Lucas Collection - page 39; Boudewijn Neuteboom - page 177; Cindy Ray - pages 122, 124, 127, 171; Stefan Richter - pages 19, 258, 264; Sheree Rose - page 263; Tattoo Club of Japan - pages 72, 94, 95, 96, 103; Richard Todd - page 90; Skip Williams - page 18; Chris Wroblewski - pages 72, 73, 120, 176, 201, 203, 216, 220, 222, 224, 225, 226, 227, 229, 261, 264, 265, 269; John Wyatt - page 72.

Additional Photographic Credits

De Luca S. (Ed) L'Asino Ela Zebra. Rome. De Luca Editore. 1985. Pages 47, 51, 181, 183, 185, 186, 188, 189, 103, 257. International Tattoo Magazine. Pages 104, 211. Rubin A. (Ed). Marks of Civilisation. Los Angeles. Museum of Cultural History. 1988. Pages 25, 26, 27, 31, 37, 44, 45, 46, 47, 56, 90, 100. Tattoo Archive. Pages 26, 37, 49, 50, 51. Tuttle J and L (Eds) Tattoo Historian. Pages 29, 40, 44, 52, 54, 55, 58, 59, 115, 119, 122, 211, 215, 216, 218, 219.

Additional Illustrations

Hardy D. E. Eye Tattooed America. Hawaii. Hardy Marks Publications. 1993. Pages 182, 243, 248, 252, Vale V & Juno A. (Eds). Modern Primitives. San Francisco. RE/Search Publications. 1990. Page 262. Norman Rockwell - page 244.

A special thanks to the magazines that help keep you up to date with the World of Tattooing.
International Tattoo, Skin Art. Tattoo, Australian Tattoo, Tattoos for Men, Australian Easyriders.

THE TATTOO

Tony Cohen

With text by
Geoff Gaylard
and
Christopher Wright

OUTBACK
PRINT

First published in 1994 by Adrian Savvas
New edition paperback published 2000
Copyright © Adrian Savvas 2000

Published by Outback Print, Unit 2, 98 Spit Rd, Mosman. NSW
Telephone 02 9960 8331

Text Geoff Gaylard/ Chris Wright
ISBN 0 949155 28 4

Contents

This book represents thirty
years collecting and is
dedicated to Doc Price -
who showed me the ropes
and got me started.

Acknowledgements

Without Jenny, Brett and Brooke, this book would still just be a pile of paper. Thanks for your help.

From the Publisher
For Marion

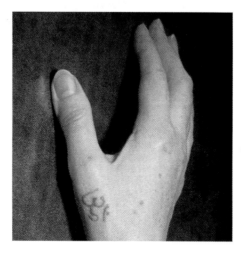

The Om
From Hinduism meaning
the Vibration of the
Universe or the sound of
the Cosmos.

Preface

The year was 1969, I was tattooing in my father's garage. Not very professional, not very comfortable, but clean. It had to do. I had several old tattoo machines, acquired underground, for a paltry sum of money. Designs consisting of the run-of-the-mill, everyone had-them type stuff. But at this time in the history of tattooing in Australia there was maybe only three or four studios in the whole of New South Wales, maybe a few others in Melbourne, possibly two in Brisbane.

Nobody to teach you. Working on friends for free, learning how to work skin, experimenting with colours. It doesn't fall in your lap. Things like getting electrocuted when machines fail. Dismantling transformers to find out why. Trying to find out why colours didn't stay in the skin when applied. Why do things break down? Needles that fall from the ends of nozzles? Why do they bleed so much? I didn't know.

There's no manual, no teacher, no Kung-fu master, saying stand this way, hold your arms up, hold your hands up. None of that, just a young fellow, like many, trying to make his mark in the world. So you go back to the source. You get another tattoo from your favourite tattoo man. This being Alex Chater. Long-standing Sydney tattoo artist for many years. The hero of thousands of young men. The father image. You watch everything he does. He won't tell you nothing, no-one in their right minds would, it's his bread and butter. He doesn't want some jerk to open up next door or down the street. He has everything under control. Some master in a faraway land had shown him the ropes.

Tony Cohen

ROD STEIGER AND CLAIRE BLOOM

Don't dare stare at

THE ILLUSTRATED MAN x

RAY BRADBURY'S masterpiece of the supernatural!

Co-Starring
ROBERT DRIVAS Also Starring DON DUBBINS · JASON EVERS · Music by Jerry Goldsmith · Produced by HOWARD B. KREITSEK and TED MANN · Screenplay by HOWARD B. KREITSEK · Directed by JACK SMIGHT

TECHNICOLOR® PANAVISION® A WARNER BROS.-SEVEN ARTS RELEASE W
through Warner–Pathé

Tony Cohen with "Miss
Nude Australia 1992".
She's wearing body paint,
not tattoos.

Tony Cohen: The Other Illustrated Man

One of Australia's best known tattooists, Tony Cohen has also built up an international reputation. Over the years he has worked from a number of locations, both in Sydney and Melbourne, but it is his *Illustrated Man* studios which are the best known. First opened in Sydney's famous Kings Cross, and now situated in Elizabeth Street, they have attracted clients from around the world keen to make use of Tony's skills.

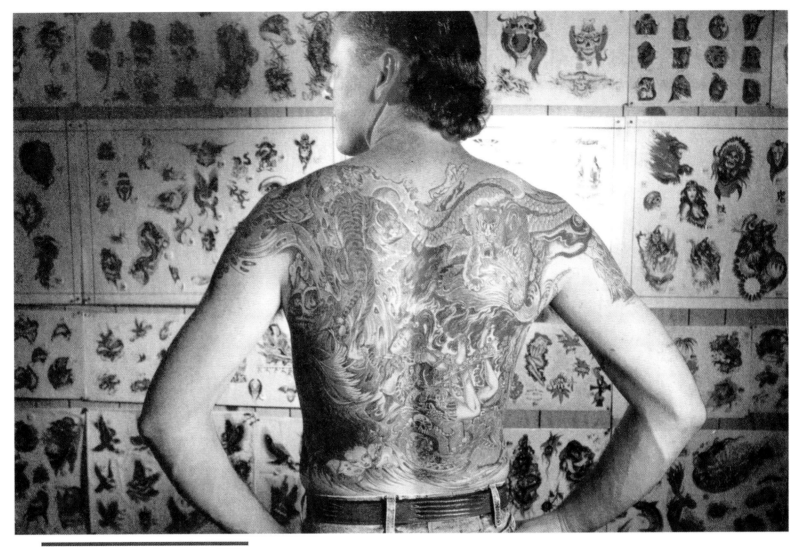

The *Good Weekend*, **January 9, 1988.**

ATTOO is a collaborative effort. Geoff Gaylard researched and wrote most of the text. Tony Cohen wrote the *Preface*, but more importantly most of the photographs and illustrations came from Tony's extensive collection of tattoo memorabilia.

Tony is probably Australia's best known tattooist having been in business for more years than he'd probably care to admit, but it's about thirty. His studio, *The Illustrated Man,* was a William Street, Sydney, landmark for many years. He has also had studios in Manly and St. Kilda, in Melbourne, and he now works from a shop on Elizabeth Street, one of Sydney's main thoroughfares, near Central Railway.

It's a long way from the traditional dockside location of the old-time tattoo parlours. But then Tony Cohen is a long way from being an old-time tattooist. This is his story in his own words:

The seed was planted. It was 1956, the year of Rock 'n' Roll, sideburns, motorcycles, Elvis Presley and all the good things. In the mind of a scrawny nine-year old kid, just recovering from a horrific traffic accident where a truck came off second best.

First visions: An uncle, Roy by name, sported several images on his huge arms. "What are those things?" I pestered, I wanted to know - bad! "Where did you get them from?" "Who did them?" *Why*? was never a question, yet it is the most common one, one is confronted with when meeting a non-tattooed person.

There was no *why* - who cared? After all, it was his body. I wasn't silly enough to say I didn't like them, they were fascinating and intriguing. Palm trees, hula girls, exotic faraway places with names like, Cairo, Egypt - "been theres" as we call them now. He displayed them proudly. Marks of distinction.

Who were such men? Freshly returned home from wars, battles, trauma, from far-off places on the other side of the world, did their wives or friends say "What the hell did you go and mark yourself up like that for, hey?" These were real men who fought for our country. Were they classed as criminals, low-lifes or drop-outs? No, these were the people who carried our flag and answered the call. You didn't see wimps sporting tattoos in those times. These men came back with their medals, ribbons, badges and proudly dis-

(Above) Tony Cohen in his *Illustrated Man* studio, with some of the thousands of his flashes on display. It's your choice.

played them with nothing to hide; we were free. I thought that even alongside my father, this man was special.

Did tattoos on soldiers and sailors make them any stronger or tougher? No way. They had a job to do and they did it: *Save Australia*. Thousands of men and women go the mark. How much ink along with souls was lost with some of the people forever? In the great wars and battles of centuries gone by, they marked themselves in some way, the men at least, from the beginning. A loved ones's name; places travelled, one didn't question these people; why did they do it? Were they all crazy? Well, maybe a little. Were they all held down, tied up and tattooed against their will? No way. Was it an on-the-spot decision, when so many got several? No. They were put there because they wanted them. And that is the answer. And after all these years I

think it is the only one. Some may have been badly executed, some were mediocre, others were beautiful displaying brilliant colours, and splendid highlights done by expert practitioners of the Art. A lifetime of memories, good, bad or indifferent. Today the process is so extravagant, complex and unique. I'm sure in modern times that tattoo studios, if it were at all possible, would have rows and rows of warriors, common soldiers and just plain battlers, lined up for miles to get their dragons and demons emblazoned on their bodies.Battles go on. The wars are still with us. And so are the warriors.

Then there is the other side of the coin. The yin and yang. The balance, so to speak. My mother hailed from New Zealand and every so often I'd visit there. After several trips

Tony Cohen tattooing heavyweight boxer, Allan Denison - "The Tattooed Flash" in 1968.

across the Tasman on the *Monowai*, on flying boats, on the ocean liners came a growing fascination with the tattooing of the traditional Maori warriors of the past. Intricate patterns on their faces, their bodies. Tattooing taken to its extreme, as exotic as outrageous as the world has ever seen and possibly ever will see again.

These tattoos were there to scare the enemy, but finally it didn't work. The warriors were conquered, and their tattoos were outlawed from the face of the planet by the turn of the century. But the images remained, were kept alive painted by great artists, the like of Angus, d'Sainson, John Savage and the most famous of all, Gottfried Lindauer. Tattooing not as we know it today; hard time, painful, no fooling around, straight to the point. These men were hard. Hours and hours of chiseling, but it was artistic, the paintings prove it. How many people have a velvet Lindauer painting in their home? How many can afford it?

And finally after many years a man comes along who can see the potential and expands all these dreams, all this imagination and offers to teach you.

The forbidden art of tattooing.

In those days you had to learn with your eyes; the eyes are the passageway. the mind creates, the hands do the deed. And so it goes. Soon your own images become life-like. "Hey, man, that's terrific!" "How about one over there on me other arm?" "I'm going to get that eagle on my chest next week." The eagles get better, the ships come to life and the hula girls get prettier.

I can still remember tattooing a fidgety customer several years later. "Keep still," I say. Fidget, fidget, it irritates him. I'm trying to do a geisha girl. He moves at the wrong time, just as I'm doing one of the eyes, one is slightly out of place. Not that much to notice, but I'm as embarrassed as hell.

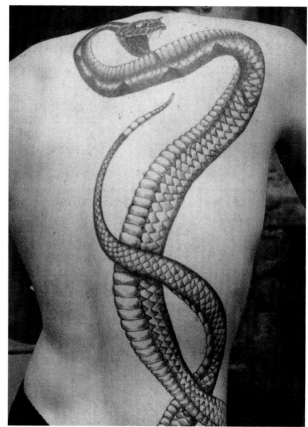

Tattoo artists have to be versatile. Just some examples of work by Tony Cohen at *The Illustrated Man*.

Tony Cohen believes in personal decoration - apart from practising what he preaches as far as tattooing is concerned, jewellery is important too.

"What the fuck," he says, "give her a pair of sunglasses." So I do, Suzi Wong with a pair of shades. "Not *bad!*" he says. Everyone's happy. And she's till running around out there somewhere enjoying the sun.

Same year. I get offered a position to work for one of the finest tattoo artists I've ever met. By the name of Darryl Morris, who has set up in the heart of Army land. This man has forgotten more about tattooing than most. And he passes it on, the way it should be, and we work hard. These are the days where for ten bob (one dollar) you could have tattooed *Blood Group A Positive.* I hope we saved some lives. Probably psychologically, more than anything else, but it is still there in an emergency. Other tattoos, the likes of *Allergic to Penicillin,* your regiment, a name, Australiana, kangaroos, crossed bayonets, bulldogs, drunken cats, kegs of beer, ships, tanks, *Mother,* Hearts and Roses, plus *God Save The Queen.* You name it, we did it. And much more, forever to fade away into oblivion.

Then there's the long hours, waiting and waiting. They all come in at once, full of juice. A dozen comrades, all to watch a mate get his first tattoo, a "virgin". He passes out instantly as soon as the needle touches his arm., too much booze, everyone laughs, but no-one else will commit himself to the test. They come back on their own, later, no crowd, no witness, no problem. "What the hell was all the fuss about," they say, "can't even feel it. "Stage fright, " we say. "Nerves. Trying to impress everyone." "You don't need to get all liquored up to get tattoos, it's easy. See you next payday."

When the Vietnam War was on, miles of tattooed skin would have left this country and most of it came back. The studios were buzzing, thousands of US troops hit the cross, taking back Wally Hammond's colourful tattoos to all parts of the world. Sydney roared.

We didn't see many at Liverpool on the outskirts, just a few. Kings Cross was where it was at. Apart from ourselves, in these times Sydney had Dutchy Cornellison, Wally Hammond, Bob and Peter, Max Chater. Names that will go down in tattoo history and be talked about over sunday dinners, barbecues, and the conventions for many years to come.

Darryl Morris revolutionised tattooing in Australia. Bold, colourful, solid tattooing made to last. Before this was the era of red and green eagles with dots for wings, roses that looked like cabbages and shapeless women. He teaches how to shade, do realistic tattoos. Tattoos you can see from across the street and know who done 'em.

I worked for him for approximately two years. He came from the old Les Skuse style of tattooing in the Motherland. He would have done more large back-pieces, probably, than anyone else in the country. A country that boasted of famous tattoo artists like Cash Cooper, Jock, Rich Mingins, Terry Wrigley, Jeff Baker, Ron Ackers and inspiring up-and-coming artists like Terry Roberts, Danny Skuse and Mickey Sharpz.

And there were other names. Who will continue fine art in England? Too many to name.

After this era, Darryl no longer happy in Australia, decided to go home and departed on an ocean liner for a long trip and well-needed rest. As I was only working part-time, Darryl decided to bring Dutchy from Manly to Liverpool to continue the business, which he did successfully for many, many years. By this time I had moved to the outer Western suburbs at St. Mary's. I was still working part-time, gaining experience, laying the foundation for a future reputation. St. Mary's was cheap in those days, you could rent a shop for $10 a week and buy a house for $7,000. But it was still hard work. Truck driving by day, tattooing by night.

Tattooed by Tony Cohen.
1994.

Tattooed by Tony Cohen.
1976.

Design courtesy Bon Ten, Japan.

With thanks to Ian "Barney" Barnwell. Tattooed 1977.

Four years later it's time to move on. Kings Cross looks good. Lots of experience to be gained up there. Also lots of pitfalls. Long hours, till three or four in the morning, no home-life, just work. Putting up with countless drunks and yahoos.

I'm working with Tom Baker, an excellent artist and painter. We have several locations. Then in 1974 I decided to go overseas. First stop was L.A. which expanded the mind so much. Places like San Diego, L.A. and San Francisco. Tattoo shops by the dozen. Artists like Lyle Tuttle, Doc Webb, Ed Hardy, Cliff Raven, Pat Martynuick, heaps of others, with fine studios. What an unbelievable business to be in, and most of all, different. Different layouts, different ideas, different flash, and I met some fantastic people. And discovered a great drive to come back to Australia and go out on my own.

I moved on to the United Kingdom and worked some more for Darryl in Plymouth, Devon. A city with so much history. And met many of the artists I had heard so much about. All the time acquiring my own little souvenirs. Getting tattooed by Rusty Skuse, the most famous female tattooist of the day, and George Bone, one of the most tattooed men in the world, who made the *Guiness Book Of Records* several times. I came back to Australia and worked

at Kings Cross for a short while, then I worked with Dutchy Cornellison, while in the process of opening up Oceanside Tattooing at Manly Beach. A great era.

I was told I'd never make it. "You'll go broke. People on the North Shore won't get tattooed." And I proved them wrong. The Oceanside Tattoo was very successful. The shop was revolutionary for its day. Big, roomy and lots of art for people to choose from. And being on the beach, probably the best position anywhere in Australia. Many tourists and servicemen. The word carries. This is the first time I started to get international customers. Germany, U.S.A., France, England, just on reputation. Not because I was in a red-light district, with strip clubs, hookers and bars to drag clients into the area. Most red-light districts throughout the world have at least one tattoo studio, or several. These are obviously one of the best places to set up if you don't want to put any groundwork into the craft.

I find it hard to believe that there would be a red-light district anywhere without a couple of tattoo studios. The abundance of studios in these areas helps the learning process as many of the most famous tattooists work from them and have clients who are just plain tourists, habitual travellers and servicemen and carry their tattoos to all parts of the world, so fine art spreads.

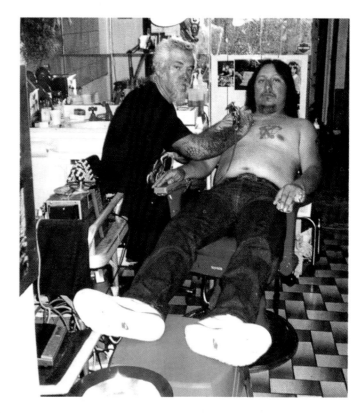

The Illustrated Man, **Elizabeth Street, Sydney.**

You could tell who was good and who was not. Some artists stayed the same, others improved slowly, others over-night. Sometimes you could tell where people had been and exactly who did the artwork, as tattooists everywhere mainly have their own style. It was another era.

Around the mid-seventies came a great influx of "amateur" tattooists, literally thousands world-wide. The main reason for this being the tattoo conventions. At the first of these, the Gatherings Of The Clan, so to say, people's awareness became more and more. At some of these conventions, supplies were sold to the public. The closed shop was now open. People who were fans became tattooists. And the equipment became more accessible to the general public. The day of the "born" tattooist was over.

This had its good and bad points. For every good and successful tattoo artist that lasted, hundreds fell by the wayside to become collectors again. The good point being that, as competition became so much tougher, the true tattoo artist emerged from the cocoon. The quality of work became outstanding. The best became even better. Those who couldn't create disappeared into the oblivion of the back alleys and backyards.

Backyarders became the scourge of the professional tattoo artist, as people put their backbone into it, spent money on sterilisers, the finest equipment and elaborate studios, not afraid to pay the rent and advertise their honourable profession. Public awareness had come of age.

The wowsers still put it down and always will. Tattoo artists are still a minority, but they are here to stay, from the beginning to the end. When a man makes his mark from the North Pole to a rose on a fine lady's bosom, that mark is there to stay. One has only to attend international tattoo conventions to see the masterpieces that are created on skin. The camaraderie, the good feelings and good karma. Friendships being renewed after years of not meeting and not seeing.

From Manly we moved onto Melbourne. Not such a good move, the time wasn't right. I set up a shop with Danny Robinson and we worked hard. Danny who, in my mind, is probably one of the greatest tattoo artists that has ever drawn breath. We put so much work into the shop and this again in itself was different. A unique studio. Completely different layout, probably the most art to pick from in any shop yet. But the powers that be could not see us working together; they had other ideas. Even though we worked together well and had good times, Sydney did not seem all that far away.

Nineteen Eighty One saw the birth of *The Illustrated Man* Studio. A busy studio, catering for clients of all discriminations. This led to television shows, interviews by the dozens, radio interviews, books, magazines. We tattooed the right people and were accepted, not just another tattoo studio, but one where customers could fill their needs, get almost whatever they wanted, from out of their own imaginations,

For some reason screaming eagles seem to bring out the best in tattoo artists. This fine example, with its delicate colour renderings on an upper leg.

to off-the-wall or just the same as dad had. Wherever they wanted it, which is extremely important. Gone are the days of Popeyes, Hot Stuff and Tweety Birds, but they still get done, they are still needed.

People come in nervous, full of stories they've heard, how much it hurts, the pain, the blood. Stories of bravado, told by former patrons who passed the test without fear. "You'll pass out," they've been told, and they're a bit fearful. But they're here for a reason.

The process is over. They are changed. no longer nervous. Extremely happy, in a new frame of mind. They are even able to watch the whole thing being done. The mystical tattoo artist doesn't harm them. He's not such a bad guy after all. The majority of tattooees are first-timers and many of them will return to expand on their personal art. And it **is** their art. Not for the world, but for one's own self and for those to whom they wish to show, or those who wish to keep it entirely to themselves.

The art of tattoo has been discussed, put down, praised, distorted on all sorts of media, written about in newspapers, periodicals and displayed on TV shows and the movies, but I believe it can never be fully explained, except by the tattoo artists themselves. In trying to upgrade the image of our art, this book is dedicated to the myriad of artists throughout the world who strive to do fine work and impress the general public with their prowess in laying down the ink, and also all their fans and supporters, who, without acknow-ledgment, none of this would be at all possible.

May your colours never fade.

Tony Cohen. Sydney. 1994.

Tony Cohen at work on a client's leg at *The Illustrated Man.* **(Opposite) Eagles are among the most popular subject for tattoos.**

Nineteenth century Maori
Chieftain, Te Hira Te Kawau.

TATTOOING: ORIGINS

There are very few countries that have not contributed to the development of modern tattooing, but the art is as old as civilisation. When our ancestors sat around the fires in their caves they probably experimented with tattooing one another. To give them an edge over their enemies, or the animals they hunted. Just when it started we don't know. It can be traced back to Ancient Egypt over four thousand years ago, but that is no reason to suppose that the Egyptians invented tattooing. It's origins are as mysterious as the ways in which it has survived, despite more than one attempt at official suppression.

Despite the comparatively simple technology involved, the forms of tattoo range from the simple patterns made up of dots and lines, typical (for example) of early Egypt and Peru, the Islamic world and north-west India - to the highly stylised, stark black geometric shapes of Indonesia, Micronesia and Polynesia, to the large scale richly pictorial tradition of Japan. The same technique and conceptual framework can produce strikingly different results, with correspondingly divergent meanings and functions, even among people who share a common heritage.

Tattoos with explicit religious associations, as in Coptic Christianity are frequent, occurring in some branches of Buddhism and among Hindus and tribal people in some parts of India. The religious associations may be coupled with the idea that one's tattoos, inalienable in this life, can be bartered to accomplish the transition to the afterlife. A related tradition encompasses designs intended to protect against illness or other misfortune. Throughout the Islamic world, tattooed charms warded off the evil eye and Hawaiian warriors wore tattoos to protect them in battle.

Tattoos also occur as emblems of accomplishment - for example, among Inuit whaling captains and head-takers in Indonesia and Iran Jaya. They may be hallmarks of a traditional way of life. Marking the skin may indicate group membership, or may possibly record significant events in the life of an individual, including initiation, nubility, and marriage. Distinctive tattoos were put on to memorialise a deceased relative (Hawaii), and tattoos often referred to vocation, as among Japanese firemen and female musicians, dancers and courtesans in ancient Egypt.

Tattoos and scarification in some early Japanese examples show a willingness to endure pain in order to please a lover. Some early societies considered the record of suffering accrued religious merit to the wearer.

The common perceptions to irreversible body art are predominantly negative, arousing strong feelings from outsiders - usually fascination blended with repugnance.

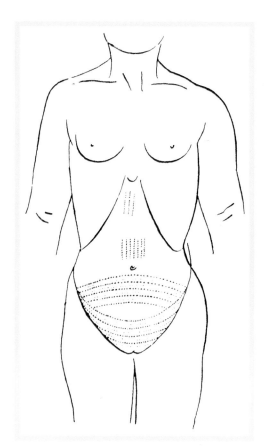

(Left) Pattern of tattoos on an Egyptian mummy from the Middle Kingdom, about 2,000BC.
(Above) Images of Bes used as tattoo motifs during the New Kingdom about 1,000BC.

(Above) A Moko image used as a signature on a deed in New Zealand in 1840.
(Right) Full body tattoo of a Polynesian warrior.

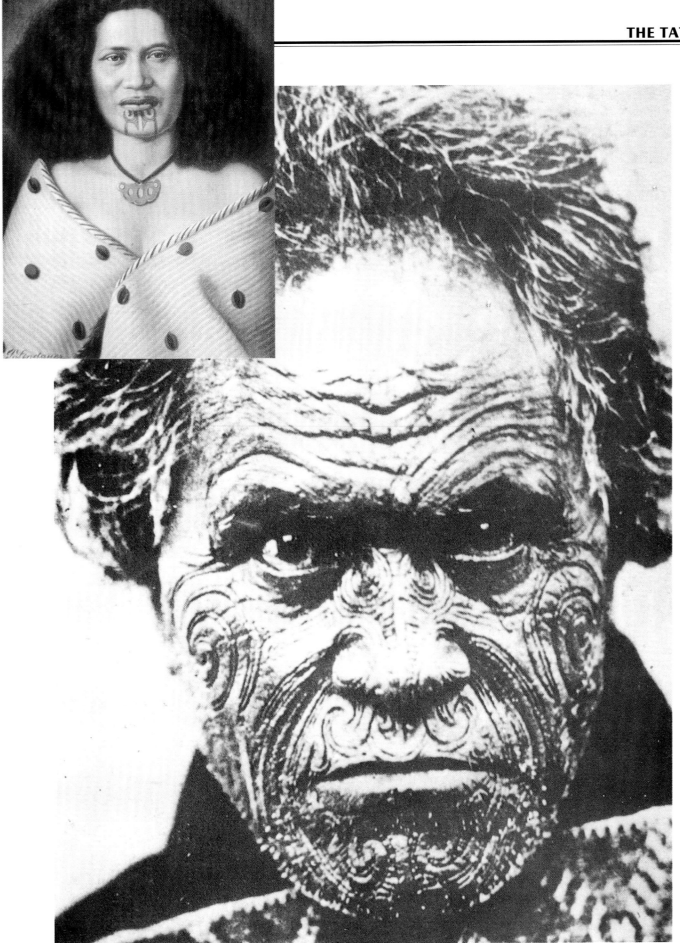

(Top) Maori woman, Raiha Reretu with distinctive facial tattoo.
(Bottom) Rauperaha, Maori chief at the massacre of Wairam in 1867.

Samoan lower body tattoo. While these are tattooed in a single colour they are among the most attractive of traditional tattoos.

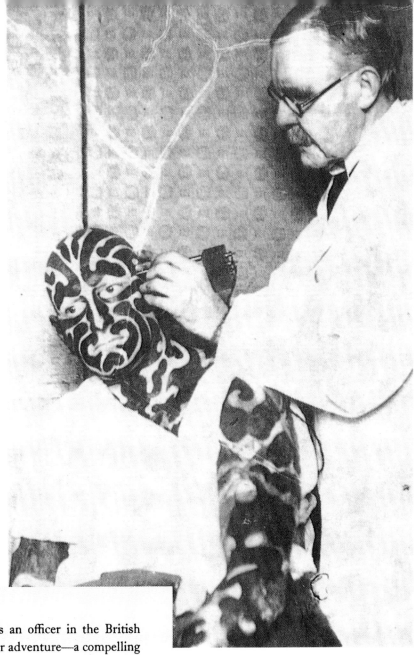

Horace Ridler -The Great Omi - had himself tattooed by George Burchett in 1934, specifically as a circus attraction. Turning a man into a zebra took 150 hours of tattooing and cost 100 pounds.

THE GREAT
OMI

OMI is unique ! After 12 years an officer in the British Army he retired with a longing for adventure—a compelling desire for the unusual, the barbaric and fantastic—and a wonderful plan to satisfy it all—a plan to have himself transformed—for life—into a being utterly sensational, thrilling and breathtaking ! So it began.

Omi was fortunate in finding skilled plastic surgeons, expert native tattooers, a dentist, a vet.—all eager to operate and create in him the appearance of some fabulous grotesque monster from another world ! They did their work well. No part of it can ever be undone ! !

The amazing head and face of Omi is a masterpiece of savage art ! Massive dark-blue stripes and curves and whirls wriggle and twist and cover from shoulders to crown ! Then — — ! Blue ears—pierced with barbaric ivory spikes ! Fierce ivory tusk right through the nose ! Sharp-pointed teeth like canine fangs ! Hands covered with fantastic curves and stripes ! Nails like blood-red talons—long—curved—sharp ! Arms—legs—body—all covered with strange dark-blue shapes ! Never before has a man been so drastically transformed ! ! And for life ! ! !

Now Omi is presented to the world. Still handsome—but barbaric. Now a breath-taking sensation—but still a charming personality with a gentle English voice. For ever — — Amazing ! Thrilling ! ! And unforgettable ! ! !

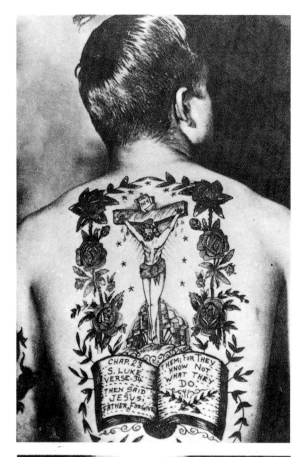

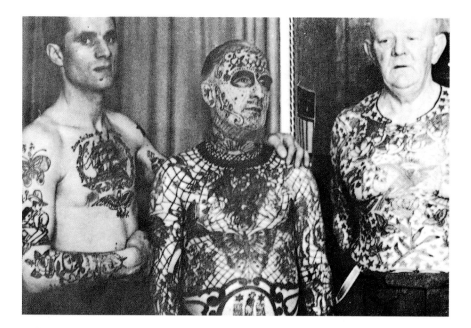

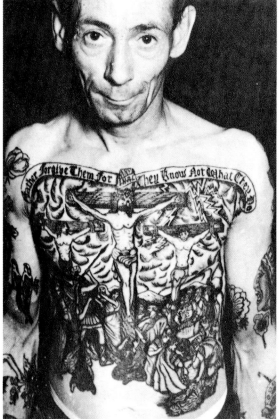

Selection of heavily tattooed men and women from the Tony Cohen Collection.

**Ancient Egyptian tattooed mummified
hand, dated around 4,000BC.**

The oldest record of tattooing in human history dates back 4,500 years to ancient Egypt. The first incontrovertible evidence being the actual tattoo preserved on the mummy of a woman named Amunet, who served as a priestess of the goddess Hathor, about 2160-1994 B.C. Her tattoos comprise a series of abstract patterns of individual dots and dashes randomly placed on the body. An elliptical pattern of dots and dashes is found on the lower abdomen beneath the navel. Parallel lines of the same pattern are found on the mummy's thighs and arms.

Excavators at Aksha uncovered a number of Nubian mummies from the fourth century B.C. (both adolescent and adult) women with blue or blue-black tattoos in precisely the same configurations as that of the mummy of Amunet.

Tattoo became firmly established within the cultural traditions of Egypt from 1550 B.C. onwards. During this time tattoo continues to be reserved exclusively for women but it is dramatically transformed. The abstract geometric forms now give way to representations of the god Bes, a curious deity associated with the household, and guardian of revelry and unbridled cavorting.

The Egyptians appear to have borrowed the form of tattooing from the Nubians. They (the Egyptians) appear to have regarded the tattoo as one of several vehicles by which the pro-creative powers of the deceased could be revived.

Reserved exclusively for women, the tattoo of the Egyptian New Kingdom could at once be imbued with either religious or secular overtones. The duality of function which categorises the Egyptian tattoo continues to serve modern societies' diverse needs and interests in a similar fashion.

Scholars today often generalise and inaccurately label the ancient Egyptians "chauvinists" or "sexist" as the origins of Egyptian tattooing was a predominantly male-oriented view of women and eroticism, inappropriate because it ignores the wider cultural context of which the tattoo is part.

The dark pigmentation of the people of sub-Saharan Africa resulted in cicatrisations (scarifications), rather than the more graphic medium of tattoo as the predominant mode of irreversibly altering the surface of the human body.

The ancient Greeks branded their slaves (doulos) with a delta, and the Romans stamped the foreheads of gladiators, convicted criminals sentenced to the arena, for easy identification. On invading Britain in 54 B.C. Julius Caesar noted with astonishment that the natives not only painted their faces with yellow weld, but wore more lasting decorations that were pricked into their skin.

In 1986, fifty well preserved non-Mongoloid bodies were discovered in northwest China. Estimated to be at least 3,000 years old, five of the bodies were tattooed with geometric patterns. Another body recovered from the border of China, Siberia and Mongolia was extensively tattooed with highly stylised animal motifs, and dated by scientists to around 500 B.C.

The great thirteenth Italian adventurer Marco Polo, reported encountering both figurative and geometric tattooing during his travels in Central Asia; "the men of the Province of Zardan'd had dark stripes tattooed on their arms and legs, which they considered a distinction or ornament".

Period photographs from the
Cohen Collection.

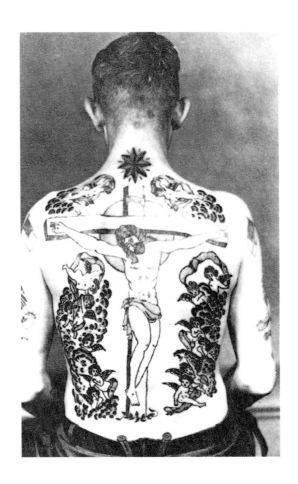

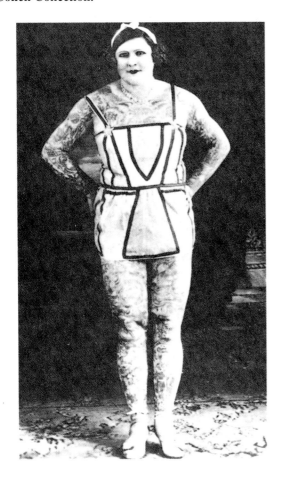

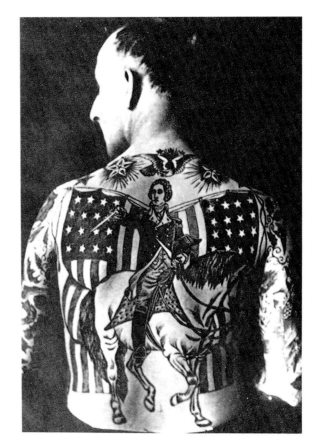

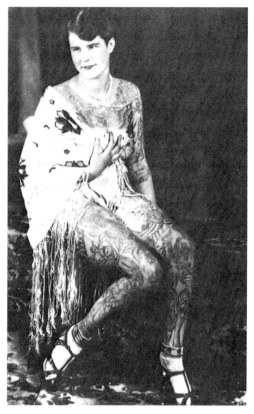

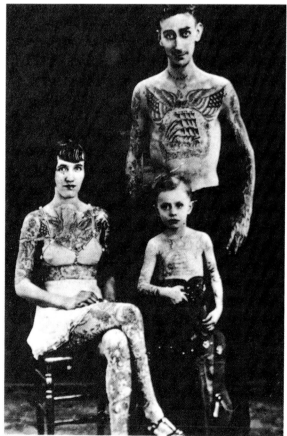

Before the introduction of minimum age laws tattooing was a family affair, although there is some doubt that the boy's are genuine.

Just another family. The idea of this leaves one speechless!

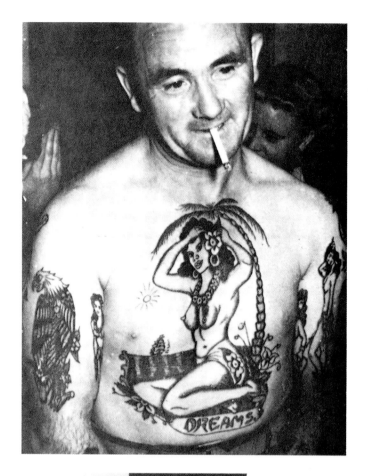

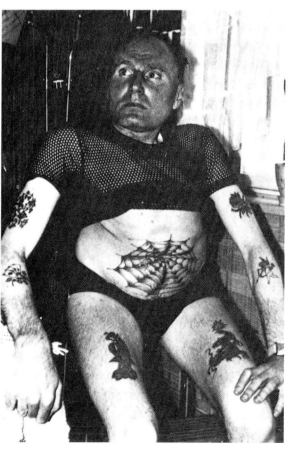

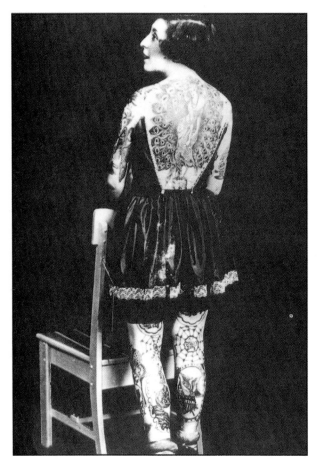

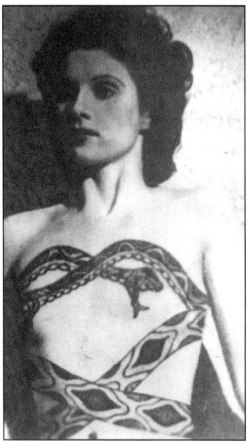

(Top) This is an example of a 'pitch' card for a European tattooed lady, Celly d'Astra. The other photographs are examples of body painting, from the Cohen Collection.

  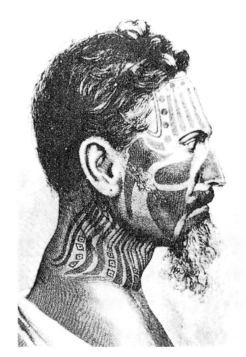

The Islands of Oceania have been the home of some of the most interesting and dramatic tattooing. The designs are ritualistic, often the expression raises Oceanic tattooing into the realm of high art.

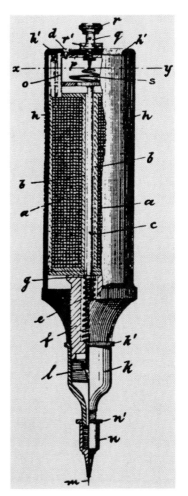

Advertisement for tattoo parlour in The Bowery, New York.

TATTOOED ROYALTY

"That high class tattooing is not degrading nor in any-wise vulgar is plainly shown by the fact that many members of our best society and persons of high standing in political as well as social circles, both ladies and gentlemen have tattoos on their bodies. Neat and artistic designs by the best tattooist and are proud of them.

When such personages as the - King of England, Emperor of Germany, King of Norway, Czar of Russia, Prince of Wales, the Bourbons of France, the "Four Hundreds" of New York, and scores of royal and social persons of high standing in Europe and America, as well as Army and Navy Officers everywhere, patronise the art, we ought not to criticise and accuse them of having consented to patronise a vulgar and barbarous custom. We could not accuse ourselves of folly if we follow the example they have set. Tattooing is not low or degrading when practiced as an art for arts sake. When royalty hangs onto a craze, you may be assured that the rest of the exclusive world of wealth and power soon follow in the same path, and annex the peculiarities of the pleasures which have given amusement to their Heroes Born in the Purple. What wonder, then, that tattooing is just now the popular pastime of the leisured world? For one of the best known men in high European circles, the Grand Duke Alexis of Russia, is most elaborately tattooed, and Prince and Princess Waldemar of Denmark, Queen Olga of Greece, King Oscar of Sweden, The Duke of York, The Grand Duke Constantine, Lady Randolph Churchill, with many others of royal and distinguished rank, have submitted themselves to the ticking, but painless and all pleasant, sensation afforded by the improved tattooing needle which is nowadays worked on a simple plan, aided by the galvanic current, the genius of the artist supplying the rest of the operation. The duke of Saxe-Coburg and Gotha, like his cousin Alexis of Russia, is another elaborately tattooed man; but even his decorations and those of other profusely tattooed men, fall short in point of quantity when compared with those marks upon the body of that Greek gentleman who was exhibited not long ago at the Royal Aquarium, whose body was completely covered with fine tattoo work, every square inch of it. Anyone meeting the Duke of Newcastle, or the Earl of Portarlington, or Sir Edmund Lechmere, in the street, would hardly realise the fact that these gentlemen are proud wearers of tattoo marks -- very much so."

This text is from a sign that hung on the wall of the W. Cail Studio in England. It is really a rather sad comment on the English class system which hasn't changed all that much since it was written about 100 years ago.

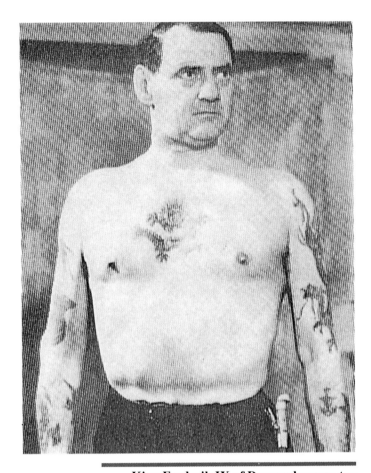

King Frederik IX of Denmark seems too young to be the same King of Denmark referred to opposite but he was certainly tattoooed - probably during his stint in the Royal Navy. During the 1940s he visited George Burchett in London for additional tattoos. He was very proud of them and showed them off for the Danish press.

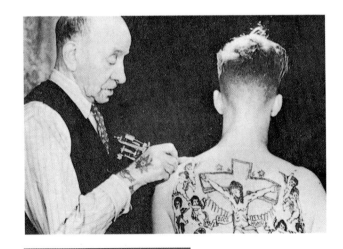

William Cail

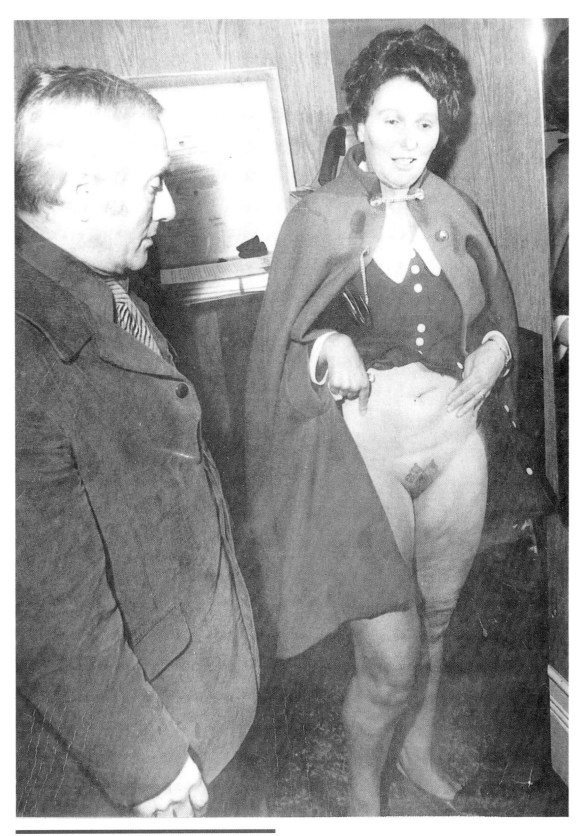

This is one of the strangest photographs in Tattoo. She seems to be a very patriotic Englishwoman - the design tattooed above her pubic hair appears to be the Union Jack and the White Ensign. The bemused man looking on is comedian the late Dick Emery.

SCARifiCATiON: BEAUTifiCATiON?

Scarification of the body is not a form of tattooing - it is caused by cutting the body and treating the wound in such a way that it will form raised scars. It is widely practised in various tribal communities around the world including Australia, but most especially in Africa. Mostly of a ritualistic nature the scarification process is used to denote that a man, or a woman, has passed certain rites of passage on the way to adulthood. The patterns of the scars can be both symbolic and individualistic indicating a person's position in the family, clan, age group and class. In some areas scarification starts when a child is only six or seven days old. Scarification isn't common outside of tribal societies but there are a number of practictioners who do cutting as an adjunct to their body piercing activities. These designs are often similar to tattoos, but are accomplished with a scalpel, rather than a tattooing needle. Unless you are a student at Heidelberg University, when it could be a duelling scar, caused by a sabre slash!

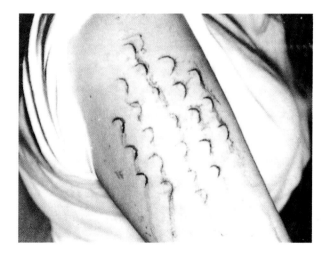

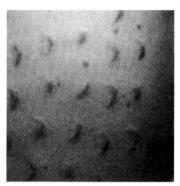

(Opposite page) Incised and raised designs on the abdomen of a pregnant woman of the Kaleri tribe, Nigeria.
(This page) Cosmetic scarification from the United States effected by cutting with a razor blade and pulling the flesh up with a fish hook.

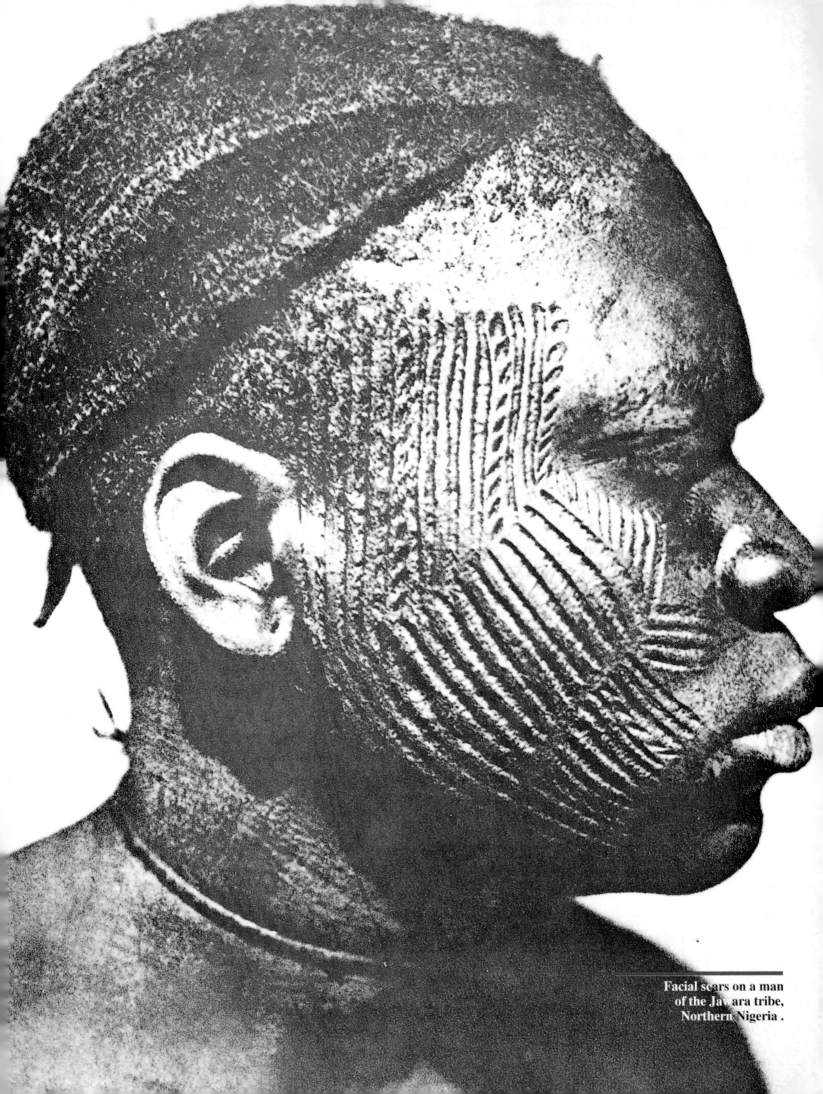

Facial scars on a man
of the Jawara tribe,
Northern Nigeria .

Taba woman from Zaire,
with facial and back scars.

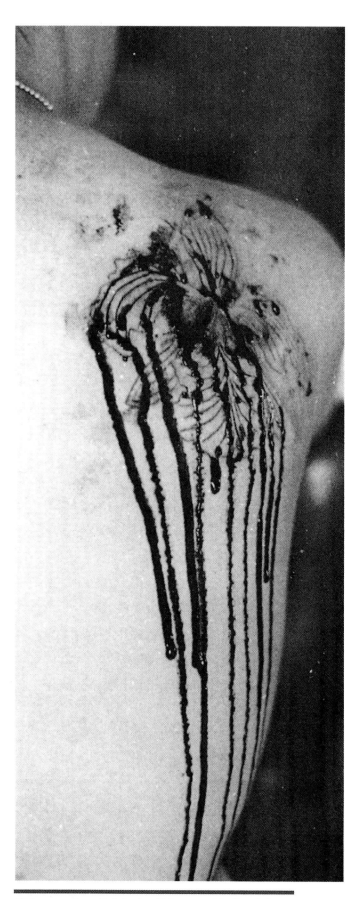

This cut, when finished will have red tattoo ink
rubbed in to form a line design created by the scar.

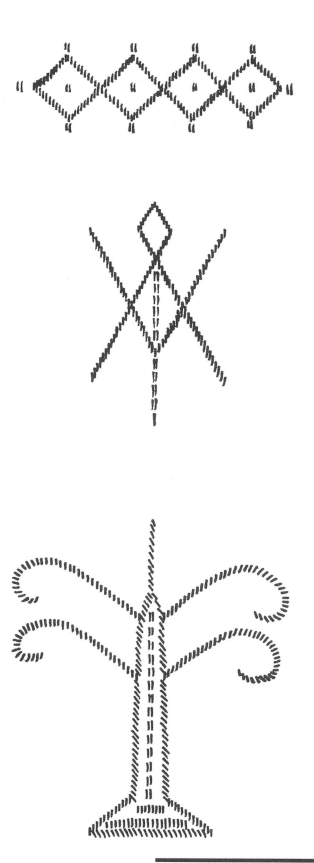

These designs are traditional
motifs of the Yoruba of
Nigeria, and are executed
with a special Y-shaped knife.

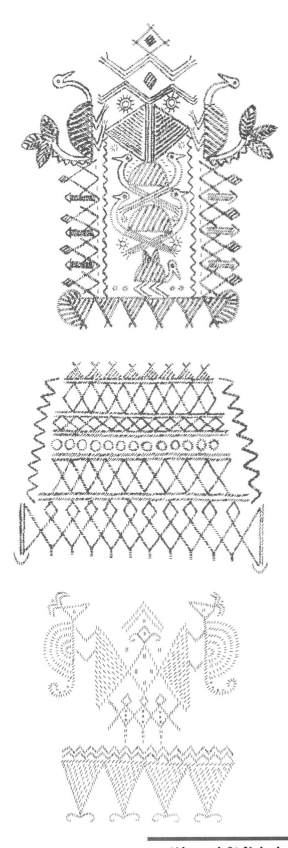

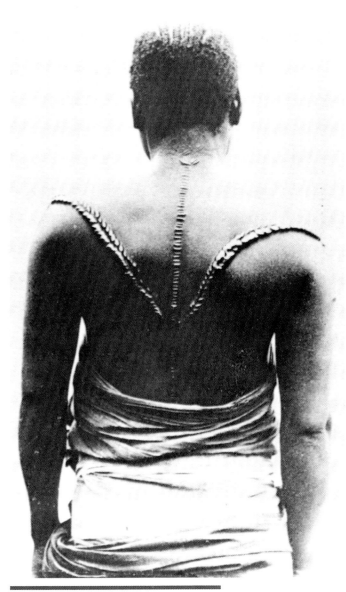

Prominent raised scars was a feature of Kondjo designs. These people live in an area between Zaire and Uganda.

(Above, left) Kolo designs from Nigeria. The one at the top features birds as well as geometric patterns.

"Arizona Jack" - Captain J. D. Franklin worked in various shows in the 1890s, as marvellous knife and battle axe thrower, as well as apparently being a pioneer Luna explorer!

Side Show Alley

Virtually from the time that Captain James Cook's second-in-command Captain Tobais Furneaux, returned to England with his tattooed South Sea Huahine Islander Omai on board the *Adventure* in 1774, tattooed men and women have been a part of the exhibition business - in special shows, in circuses and on side-show alley. The history of tattooing abounds with people who have turned their tattoos into a way of earning a living by showing them to the curious in return for a few coins. The Great Omi is an example, as is Bev Robinson, said to be the last tattooed lady to tread the boards in Australia. The pages of *The Tattoo Historian* is full of them. Some, like Omi had themselves tattooed deliberately in order to become citizens of side-show alley. Others got the tattoos first, then turned them to earning a honest, or in some cases a not-so-honest dollar.

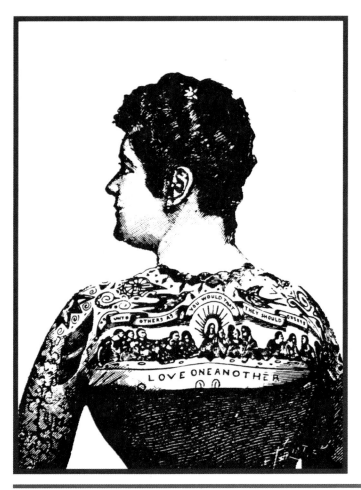

Frank and Emma DeBurgh were one of the most famous American husband and wife teams around the turn of the century. After a successful launch in Berlin around 1891 they toured extensively. Tattooed mainly with religious motifs the highlights including the 'Last Supper' and 'The Calvary'. In later years Emma grew very stout and it was reported that the Apostles in the 'Last Supper' were consequently wearing broad grins.

Captain Georges Costentenus - "The Greek Albanian" worked as a showman under the management of P.T. Barnum who is reported to have paid for his tattooing. The cards (opposite) are typical of those used to promote European tours by tattooed ladies in the last decades of the nineteenth century. There was an almost insatiable appetite for the bizzare and unusual and dozens of men and women worked in this way.

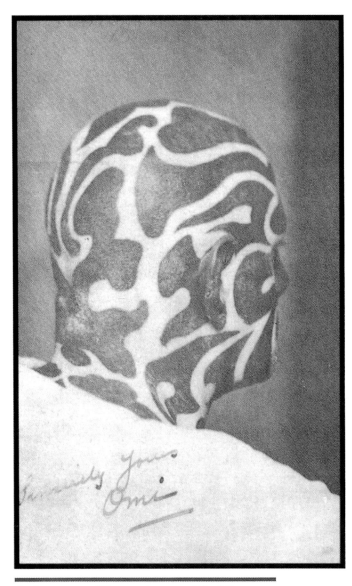

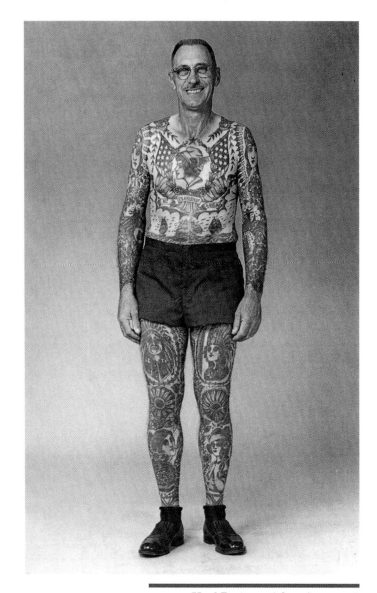

Omi was one of the most successful of the tattooed showmen from the mid thirties through to the fifties. But life on the road was not always easy, as a letter from Omi to George Burchett (the man who tattooed him) written after a tour of France in 1935 shows…"Well, I stuck it out for over three months always hoping for an improvement and always (wife and I) half dazed with want of sleep; continual travelling, long hours, sometimes 10 in the morning and on to midnight; bed at 1 in the morning, up at 6 and then 50 to 80 kilometres to the next town and so on. "…One sunday I felt too ill to work and told them (the circus management) so. They demanded a medical certificate. So I went to a doctor and had myself overhauled. He told me that I was suffering from gas poisoning caused by the urine from the lions which in that humid climate, evaporated and it was slowly poisoning me." In 1941 Omi toured Australia and New Zealand, hopefully more successfully than his French trip.

Karl Bumpus (above) was not, strictly speaking, a performer. Apparently he acquired his tattoos around 1930 with the object of working in Tom Mix's sideshow. But Mix died and the sideshow folded and Karl became a railroad man. Right) Lady Viola, 1928.

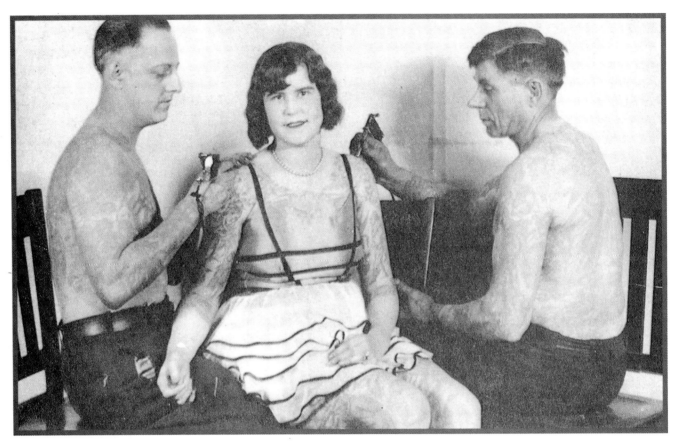

STRANGE AS IT SEEMS   By HIX

NAY, I REPENT IT --
IS AN ANAGRAM OF
PENITENTIARY!

WILLIAM E. BOICE -- 75,
HAS BEEN TOWN TREASURER
OF EGREMONT, MASS.,
FOR 48 CONSECUTIVE YEARS!
THE TOWN HAS NO DEBT

THE HUMAN
PICTURE GALLERY!

BETTY BROADBENT --
TATTOOED LADY,
IS COVERED WITH
465 DESIGNS --
IN FOUR COLORS!

MOST OF
FLORIDA'S ORANGES
DO NOT GROW
ON ORANGE TREES!

TATTOOED LADY
"It is a woman's privilege to change her mind, but I am the one woman who no longer has that privilege."

Thus philosophizes Betty Broadbent, whose pretty face vies for attention with her multi-colored, pictographic limbs and torso. "I began having myself tattooed at 16," she says, "taking six years to cover my body completely.

"Each design is entirely different. There are 465 in all, tattooed in four colors—red, blue, green and brown."
Tomorrow: The Blind Sculptor.

When she first started as a tattooed lady in show business in 1927 with the Ringling Bros. Barnum & Bailey Circus as "the youngest tattooed woman in the world", Betty Broadbent was 18. For the next forty years she appeared in numerous circuses, finally retiring in 1967. Before World War II she spent two years touring Australia and New Zealand. In the photograph above she is billed as "Betty, America's Tattooed Venus" at the Greenhalgh and Jackson Show somewhere in Australia. She also featured in a "Strange As It Seems" cartoon feature (opposite page, left) which claimed she was "covered in 465 designs in four colours". Not long before she died she was the first person elected to the Tattoo Hall Of Fame, sponsored by the San Francisco Tattoo Museum. The group of people taken on 27 August 1930 at Sells Floto Circus are the stars of the Sideshows. Betty is in the middle row at the extreme left. The giant is Texas Jim Traver and the fat lady Jolly Bertha Curtis. The lady who looks like a bird is called Koo Koo. The tattooists in the top picture are at left Joe Van Hart and right Charlie Wagner. The photo circa 1930.

As well as tattooed men and women working the sideshows, many tattooists also worked on side-show alley - some of the most famous names in tattooing did this in the early days of the century. Professor Delend (left) was just one of hundreds who plied their art for the curious and the impulsive at circuses and fairs around the world.

Major-General H. G. Robley with his collection of thirty-five Maori heads, hung on butcher's hooks and neatly arranged in a little Japanese tea-house on the lawn of an English country house around 1902.

Tattoos & The Macabre

Many people regard tattooing itself as being on the bizarre side, but there have been at least two off-shoots from the practice of tattooing that are positively ghoulish. While there have been tales of tobacco pouches made from women's breasts and lampshades made from human skin which haven't been authenticated, the heads of Maoris and whole skins of Japanese Irezumi have been collected because of their tattoos and have been placed in museums.

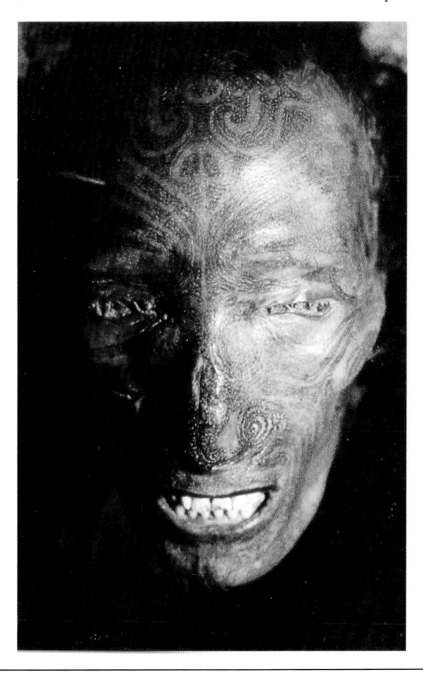

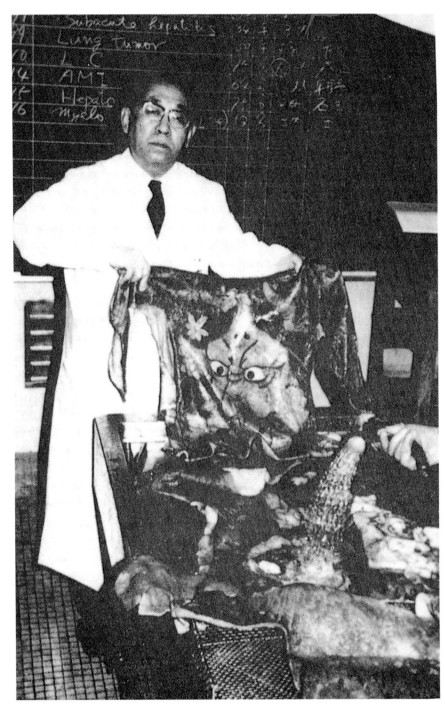

(Top and right) The Pathology Museum of the University of Tokyo has the world's largest collection of tattooed human skins. The man who started the collection Dr. Masaichi Fukushi and his son Dr. Katsunari Fukushi have concentrated on quality, preserving masterpieces of Japanese tattoo art.

(Below) This is a facial mask of a Maori chieftain cast by a British Governor of New Zealand, Sir George Gray, during the 1880s.

**Dr Fukushi with one of the
specimens in the Tokyo
University Collection.**

Adornment of the skin usually attracts some attention - but it is not always attention of a welcome kind. Perhaps because it is regarded as a curiosity, or perhaps because it is seen as uniquely artistic, tattooed skin sometimes endures in strange ways - and long past the time the bearer has joined the ranks of the deceased.

The Irezumi, a highly tattooed lower caste of Japanese society, provide an illustration of this. Since the late nineteenth century, some Irezumi with remarkable masterpieces rendered by renowned tattoo artists - and perhaps with an urge for immortality - have bequeathed their corpses to university laboratories, much in the manner of Westerners becoming organ donors. On receipt of such a donation, specially trained doctors remove the skin from the fresh cadaver in a single piece. It is then oiled and mounted, eventually in glassed and airtight frames, for display. The pathology department at Tokyo University has the largest known collection in existence; a macabre 'art gallery' of a hundred different examples.

Sometimes, however, these prized skins are not donated, but sold while the wearer is still alive! Irezumi who have fallen on hard times and urgently need money sometimes sell their skins to institutions capable of completing the preservation process. In return for cash, they then sign over the 'ownership' of their bodies after death has occurred. These institutions may then sell the preserved skin to a museum or a private collector. It is estimated that about three hundred preserved Irezumi skins are in existence within various collections. Most such skins are of elaborate full-body or half-body tattoos, sometimes decorated in the 'river' style - which leaves a strip of unadorned skin which facilitates the eventual flaying of the cadaver. Such a style

of tattooing suggests premeditation of the flaying process! This practice is discouraged more than it formerly was, by means of complicated legalities, but it is still possible to make such an arrangement. Beyond the expressed and recorded wishes of the living Irezumi subject, the consent of the entire immediate family must be obtained, and official documents must be signed and sealed. Consequently, new preserved skins are rare. Occasionally, skins may come up for auction, and they command impressive prices. One example of a half-body tattoo, sold in the early 1980s, fetched around fifty thousand American dollars.

Another illustration of the odd fate which may befall tattooed relics may be found on the other side of the globe in New Zealand. The Maori people of New Zealand practised a distinctive form of tattooing called *moko*, and frequently concentrated this adornment upon the face. In the early nineteenth century, lawless sealers and whalers frequenting the coast of New Zealand sometimes traded weapons and gunpowder for tattooed heads. Most of the preserved heads were of high-ranking warriors slain in tribal battles, although some were of captured enemies who were hastily tattooed and killed specifically for the grisly trade. The weapons they were traded for were used in more inter-tribal wars.

In May 1988, a court action instituted by the non-government Maori Council but financially guaranteed by the then New Zealand Minister for Maori Affairs, Koro Wetere, was brought against Bonham's, a British auctioneering firm., in an attempt to stop the sale of a preserved and tattooed Maori head. The Maori Council - which is dedicated to the social, economic, spiritual and cultural advancement of the Maori people - wanted the heads of their ancestors returned to their homeland for proper burial by their tribesfolk.

An estimated two hundred preserved Maori heads were known to have been collected and kept, mainly in American and British institutions, although specimens were also known to be in museums in Germany, Austria, France, Ireland and Russia. Because the museums involved argued that the tattooed head were legitimate artefacts rather than simply human remains, the National Museum of New Zealand was eventually forced to negotiate their return by swapping other artefacts on an inter-institutional basis.

As gruesome as the commercial collection of whole skins as artworks and the keeping of tattooed human heads as scientific curios undoubtedly are, perhaps even more macabre are tales of tattooed human skin being casually used in everyday objects. Stories abound in parts of America about certain frontiersmen having tobacco pouches fashioned from the tattooed breasts of Indian women, and it has always been rumoured that Hitler's mistress, Eva Braun, had a lampshade constructed from tattooed skin collected from the inmates of concentration camps. The making of such epidermal artefacts must surely rank, along with cannibalism, as among the most grossly repulsive of all human activities.

TATTOOS: DECORATIVE OR ANTISOCIAL?

People's attitudes to tattoos tend to be extreme – love, hate or fascination. To some people skin art is the most beautiful form of personal adornment possible. To the majority, however, tattoos and the people who wear them are threatening, representing a non-conformist part of society they would rather not know about, regarding them as antisocial. Still others, while they would probably never have a tattoo, are fascinated by them – both as works as art and as decorative symbols. There is no answer as to whether or not they are decorative or antisocial. Tattoos can be both. That's part of their attraction.

(Opposite page) Tony Cohen's 1994 rendition of an 1848 print by Kuniyoshi of Oniwaka Maru and the Giant Carp. (Above) Painting by Dave Smith of the William Street studio of The Illustrated Man. 1986.

Tattoos: to some people they are a mark of beauty, group identity or individuality, to others a distasteful flamboyance or disfigurement and to yet others a poorly understood taboo. Whether tattoos are seen as being decorative or appears to depend upon the time, the place and the people one associates with. Certainly they seem to be a subject about which few people are neutral; reactions still tend to be polarised and strong for such a simple matter. Undeniably, they are experiencing a resurgence; gaining in popularity, gaining recognition as a 'new' art form, and within themselves, gaining an intricacy and artistic sophistication hitherto unknown.

Sometimes the term tattoo has been loosely but incorrectly applied to the deliberate inducement of scars, but this rather more dangerous practice is more properly known as cicatrisation. Cicatrisation is most common among tribal societies and is frequently associated with puberty rites. It relies for its effect on raising of scar tissue above the level of the surrounding skin and although sometimes foreign substances are introduced into a cut to achieve this, they are of secondary importance, merely a means to the primary aim of raising a scar. Tattooing produces a permanent mark by the deliberate introduction of pigments through ruptures in the skin. The difference lies in tattooed areas generally remaining flush with the surrounding surface and being of a different colour or colours to the natural skin.

With *moko*, a highly developed form of tattooing practised by the Maori people of New Zealand, the raised

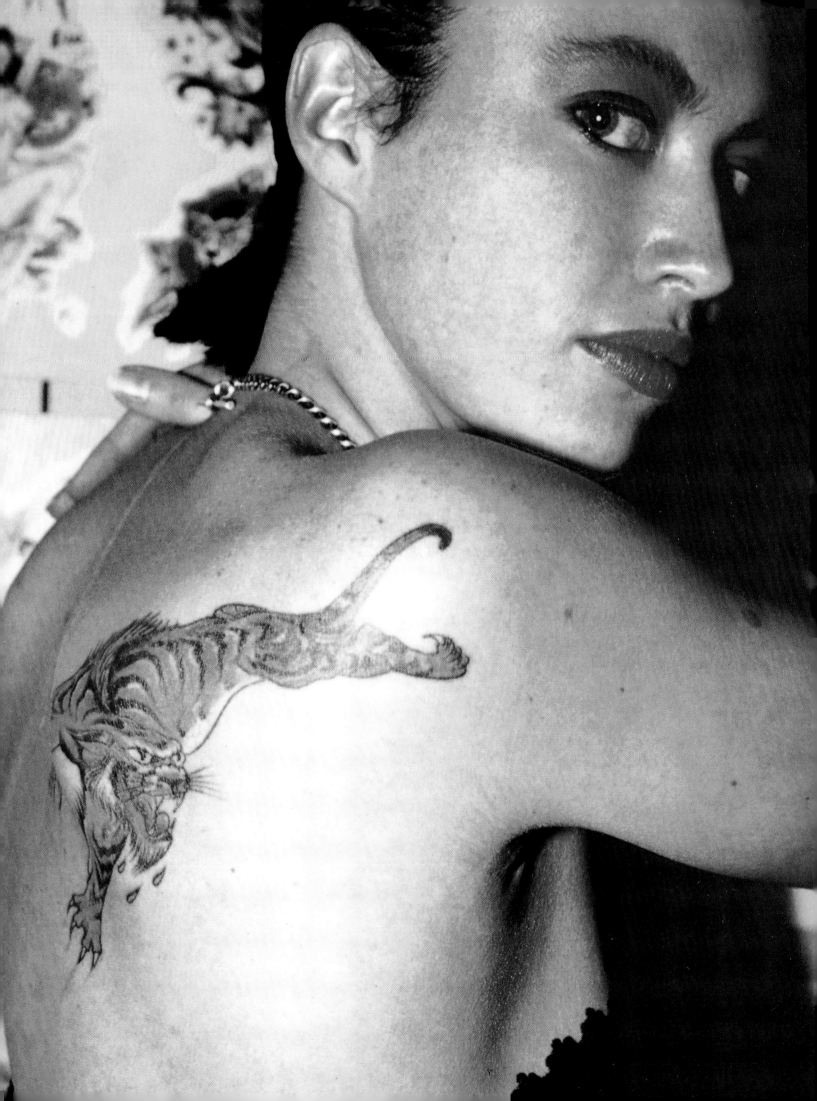

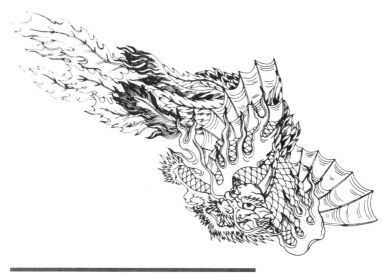

Creatures from mythology are also important in tattooing and images of creatures as diverse as dragons and centaurs appear in the portfolios of most tattoo artists. This dragon is a 'flash' illustration by Japanese tattooist, Kazuo Oguri.

The unusual has always been a part of tattooing. Images of death, horror and the grotesque are recurring themes in the work of tattooists from all parts of the world.

appearance of cicatrisation and the colouring of the tattooing was combined. This was achieved by striking a miniature bone adze into the skin, as well as introducing pigments. The resulting patterns, usually complex and curvilinear, produced shallow coloured grooves rather than raised scars. Usually, *moko* and conventional tattooing techniques were combined to form striking and remarkably sophisticated effects. This form of tattooing was unique to the Maori people and late in the last century it gave rise to the development of a gruesome and grisly trade: the exchange of heads displaying *moko* to Europeans, in return for gunpowder and weapons to be used in the interminable tribal wars.

The word 'tattoo' itself was introduced into English and other European languages from Tahiti, where it was first recorded by members of an expedition led there by Captain James Cook in 1769 - but tattoos have been around for far longer than that!

Indeed, tattoos have been found upon Egyptian mummies dating from over four thousand years ago. Some were tattooed in life - others after their death, as a form of protection from dangers expected in the spirit world. A study of the earliest classical authors reveal mention of their use by the Thracians, Greeks, Gauls, ancient Germanic tribes and ancient Britons and it is known that they were used by the Romans to permanently mark and so identify, criminals and slaves.

After the advent of Christianity tattooing was forbidden throughout most of Europe, although it persisted in the Middle East and other parts of the globe. The prohibition on tattooing came about from the theological idea that man

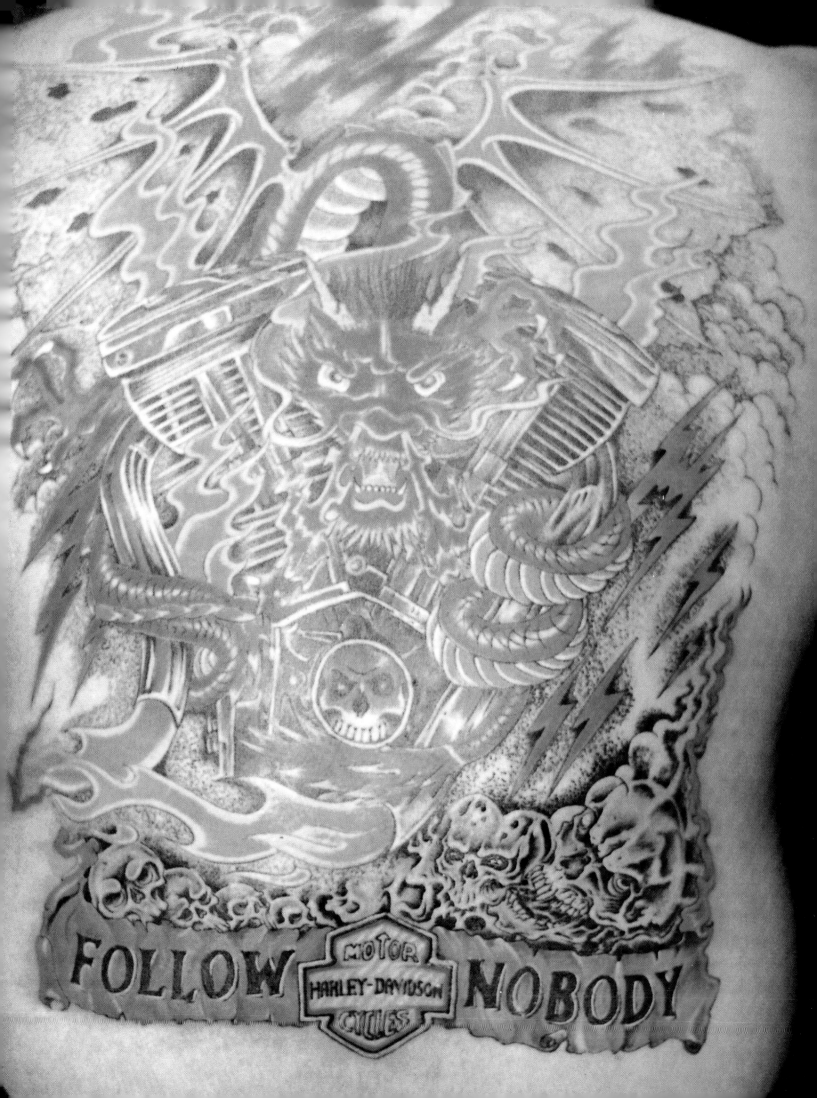

was created in God's image and that God dwelt within man as a form of earthly 'temple' - thus tattooing was interpreted as a desecration of that earthly temple. Later, when the Old Testament became commonly available, the European clergy formalised their objections to tattooing by quoting from it: "You shall not make any cuttings in your flesh on account of the dead or print any marks upon you." (Leviticus. 19:28). Other Christians disagreed: the Coptic Church encouraged the practice of having a crucifix tattooed upon initiates to publicly proclaim their beliefs.

The practice of tattooing was relatively rare among the peoples of darker skin colouration, where its effect was least noticeable and for several centuries it has also been rather rare among most of the various Chinese people . Overall, though, its occurrence has been extensive, and many characteristic national and tribal styles appeared. Designs and colours varied according to cultural influences, the pigments readily available and to a lesser extent, upon the technique used to introduce the pigments into the flesh.

In the Americas, many Indian tribes customarily tattooed either the body or the face and sometimes both. The usual technique was simple pricking with thorns or other needle-like implements such as fish bones and it was these which carried the pigment. Some of the tribes in the California region employed a technique of introducing colour into scratches and many inhabitants of colder northern climes. including American Indians, Eskimos and some of the people of Eastern Siberia made needle punctures through which a thread coated with pigment was drawn beneath the skin. Sometimes pigment was rubbed into knife slashes as was the case with the Ainu in Japan, Chontal Indians of Mexico, the Ibo of Nigeria and some of the peoples of Tunisia.

Other cultural groups employed specially designed tattooing implements. In Polynesia, Micronesia and parts of what is now Malaya, pigments were pricked into the skin by tapping with an implement shaped like a miniature rake, while in Burma a penlike brass implement with a split point and a weight on the upper end was used. The Japanese utilised needles set into a wooden handle to produce very elaborate and multicoloured designs which often covered most of the body.

Tattooing was rediscovered by the Europeans and an interest in it re-awakened, when they came into contact with the Pacific islanders and the American Indians. Tattooed Indians and islanders were transported on ships to European and American cities and exhibited at fairs and circuses, where they attracted considerable interest. Europeans who had been tattooed abroad also appeared at the same venues. Stimulated by Polynesian and Japanese examples, commercial tattoo 'parlours', where specialised 'professors' supplied designs, sprang up in port cities all over the world.

In 1891, the first electric tattooing machine was patented in the United States of America and tattooing enjoyed a brief vogue among both sexes of the British upper classes. However, it was the United States which became the chief centre of influence in tattoo designs, especially with the spread of American tattooers' pattern sheets. Tattooing prospered: the electric needles were relatively painless and the use of pattern sheets meant that an acceptable result was virtually certain, irrespective of the artistic abilities of the tattooer. The nautical, military, patriotic, romantic and religious tattoo motifs most commonly applied became similar in style and subject matter throughout the world. Sadly, the diversity and distinction of the former cultural styles of many other populations vanished at much the same rate.

Until the recent advent of lasers, which can obliterate tattoos, (although there is sometimes scarring) all tattooing was permanent. Consequently, tattoos had certain practical advantages, ones which led to them being applied as a stigma to released United States' convicts and British army deserters in the last century. During this century they were similarly used on the inmates of the Nazi concentration camps and certain Siberian prisons. This permanence also has some applications in certain special medical and veterinary circumstances (such as denoting rare blood types for people in high risk circumstances who may require blood transfusions, or for identifying neutered animals) as well as some beauticians' shops (for permanently darkening eyebrows or highlighting 'beauty spots').

Permanence also bestowed a special significance upon tattoos. Although decoration was undoubtedly the simplest and most common motive for tattooing, certain peoples believed their markings provided magical protection

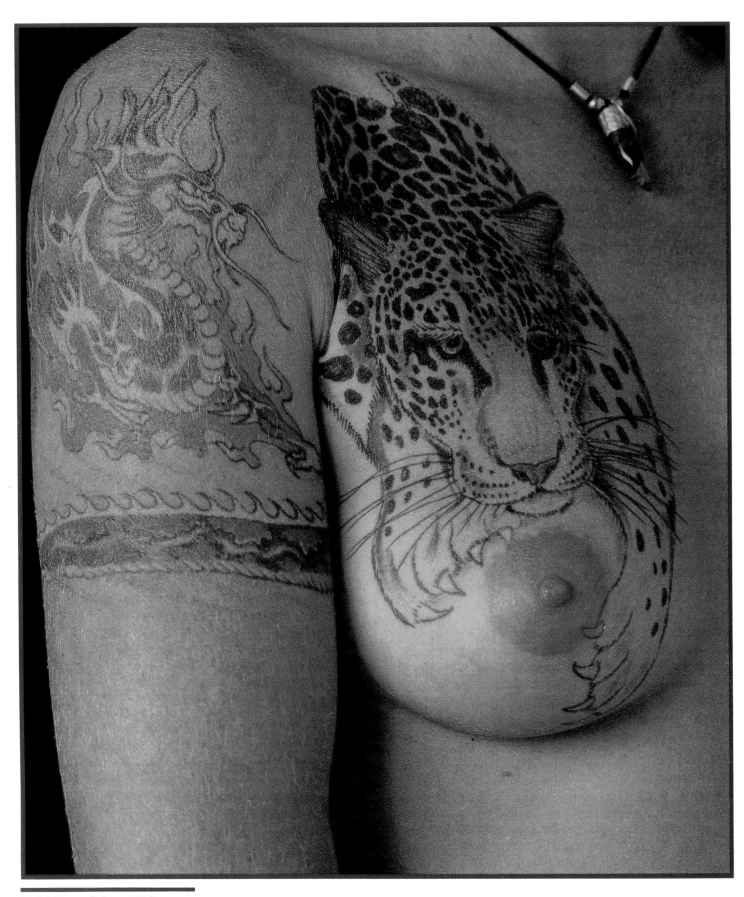

Nicki. Tony Cohen. 1993

against illness or misfortune. In other cases they served to identify a wearer's rank, status or membership of a particular group. Some tattoos still serve this purpose today: certain street gangs and motorcyclists' groups often wear tattooed insignia identifying them with their associates. Perhaps the most striking example of this use of tattooing occurs among the yakuza, a diversified Japanese criminal society very similar to the Mafia. Many yazuka initiates sport elaborate and multi-coloured tattoos, often covering most of the torso, arms and legs.

Despite tattoos being readily available within European societies since the closing years of the last century, they have never enjoyed a majority following among the most fashion conscious sections of the populace. It is true that there have been brief periods when they were in vogue for one or both sexes, but never to the extent that most people adopted them - they tended to remain a 'fringe' form of adornment. Perhaps this goes part of the way towards explaining their long-continued popularity: wearing a tattoo is seen as being a statement of individuality.

**Traditional Moko tattooing on Maori
chieftain Haora Tipa Koinaki.**

ON YOUR HEAD BE IT.

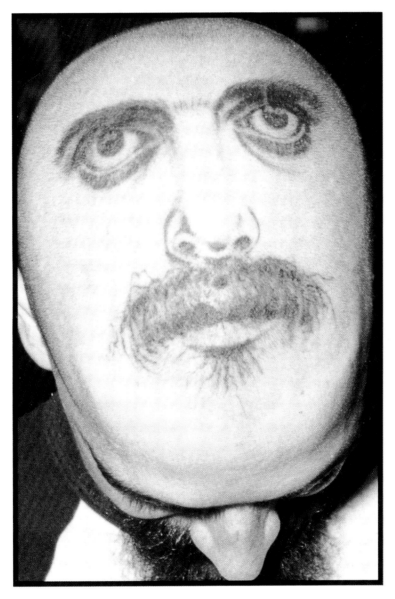

Tattoos on the top of the head are not common. Neither are full facial tattoos. However, people have been decorated on just about every part of the body and the head is no exception. The Maoris used full facial motifs to denote status, as did a number of other "primitive" peoples, so in some societies it is a sign of social acceptance. However, the man who requested that hair be tattooed on his bald head would be an eccentric anywhere. As would Omi, an out of work English army officer who decided to become tattooed as a way of guaranteeing income by him-

turning himself into a walking exhibition. Omi's tattoos were acquired rapidly to a pre-determined, and very spectacular design. Probably inspired by a zebra, Omi's black and white swirls are still striking today.

Like Omi, most people who elect to have tattoos on the face and head are making a real statement - some with more humour than others - and a real commitment to tattooing.

Like Gully Foyle in Alfred Bester's *Tiger, Tiger*, it is difficult to remain inconspicuous when you've a tiger"s head tattooed on the most prominent part of the anatomy.

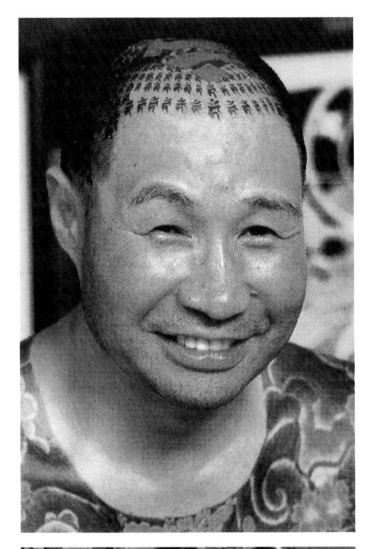

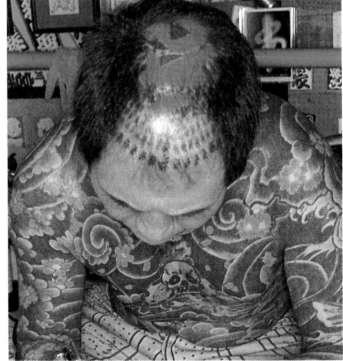

Tattoos on the head take many forms from the crude to the magnificient. It is probably the ultimate step in the pursuit of body art. Not every one wants to take it as far as Omi or a Maori chief, or make a statement like the young man (top right) or be as colourful as Mitsuaki Owada, one of Japan's most renowned tattooists, or the lady with the green hair. But for some head tattoos are irresistible, although most tattooists have a policy of not tattooing the head.

The Card & Poster Collection

Business cards are so much a part of everyday life that we seldom take much notice of them. Yet for business people they are often the front line of their relationship with their customers. Companies and individuals spend vast amounts of money ensuring that the image they project is the right one. Tattooists are no different, except that their cards are usually more imaginative than most. Just as imaginative are the posters they use to advertise their studios and events. The cards and posters are also fun to collect. Tony Cohen has been doing it for years and these examples are from his extensive collection of tattoo related material.

Stan Davies and Dudley W. Midlands

Kazou Oguri

P. J. Stevens

JOHNNY TWO THUMB TATTOO Studio SINGAPORE

TATTOOING
ST. PAULI
TATTOO STUDIO

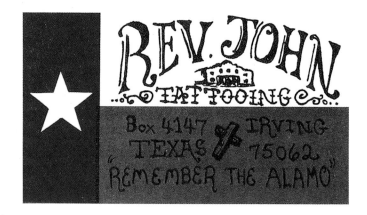

REV. JOHN TATTOOING
Box 4147 IRVING
TEXAS 75062
"REMEMBER THE ALAMO"

Ron Ackers worked for *The Illustrated Man* **1992 - 1993.**

Spider Webb

Studios Limited
112 W. 1st Street
Mt. Vernon, N.Y. 10550 U.S.A.
(914) 699-0537

Doc Graham is based in Cardiff, Wales, in the U.K.

This card dates
from about 1968.

An early card of Bill Phillips.

TATTOOING

By Paul Ortloff

121 N. Front St., Kingston, N.Y.
(Upstairs Next To Stadium Diner)
Weds. - Sat. 1 pm - 9 pm

Frank Collins

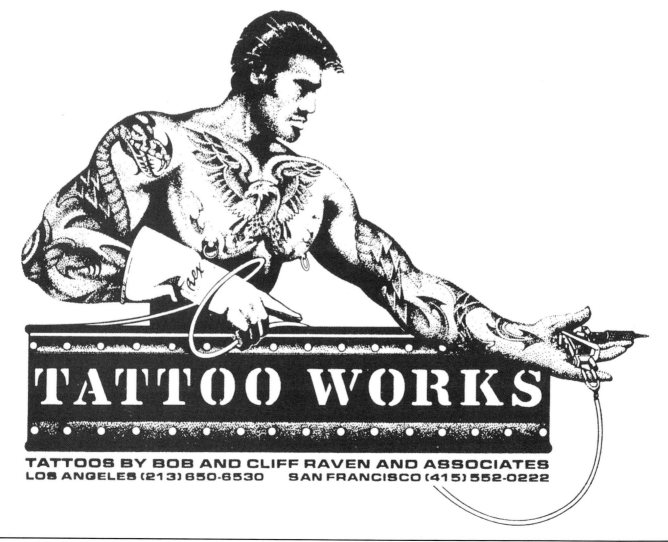

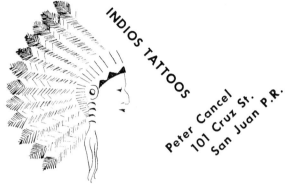
Les Bowen's original card.

Another card from an American tattoo artist.

Andre Jensen works out of Auckland Tattooing.

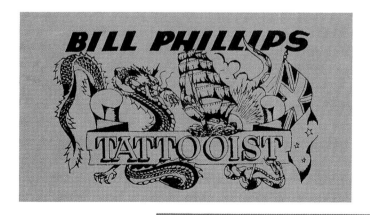

TATTOO JEFF

The card (right) is that of Jeff Jaguar
of Salisbury, Wiltshire England.

TATTOO EXPO 82

R.M.S. QUEEN MARY
LONG BEACH, CALIF.

12·13·14 November 1982

presented by Triple E Productions Inc.

Peter and Tonny De Haan.

(Right) After World War II, Sydney.

CUSTOM TATTOOING
BY Robert
Benedetti

T. Roberts also worked at
The Illustrated Man **1987 - 1991.**

NAYLAND TATTOO
STUDIO

285A Nayland Road, Stoke,
Nelson.
Phone 79-263
(Evenings & Weekends)

Tattoo Club of Japan

日本刺青倶楽部

Mitsuaki Ohwada

大和田 光 明

TATTOO DESIGN INSTITUTE
AZUMA SO 47-1 MAKADO-CHO
NAKA-KU YOKOHAMA JAPAN 〒231

文身デザイン研究所

〒231 横浜市中区間門町1の47 吾妻荘15号
TEL.(045)622—7506

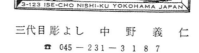

三代目彫よし 中野義仁
☎ 045－231－3187

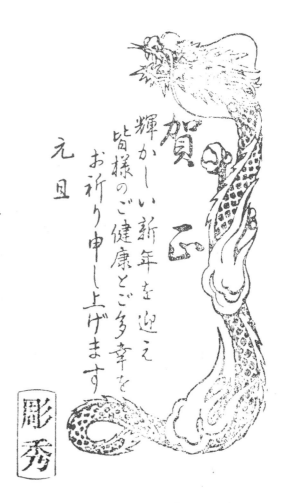

賀正
輝かしい新年を迎え
皆様のご健康とご多幸を
お祈り申し上げます
元旦

彫秀

Lyle Tuttle, Tattooist & Showman

In the Tony Cohen collection of tattoo memorabilia there is more Lyle Tuttle material than that of any other person. Perhaps it may be because he is a consumate showman as well as a highly regarded tattoo artist. He's certainly highly skilled at marketing himself. Preparing posters and postcards in addition to business cards; lecturing on university campuses; running a museum and cafe as well as his studio and exhibiting his work at galleries throughout the United States.

LYLE TUTTLE'S TATTOO ART COLLECTION

OCTOBER 7 THROUGH NOVEMBER 10, 1976

EUPHRAT GALLERY
DE ANZA COLLEGE
CUPERTINO

"IS TATTOO ART ?" Hear Lyle Tuttle, Bobby the Tattooed Lady, and Professor Mc Caffrey in person! Then help celebrate Lyle's Birthday. THURSDAY, OCTOBER 7, 8 o'clock P.M.

TATTOO

White Walls

NOVEMBER 7 ··· DECEMBER 2

san francisco state university
student union art gallery hours: m-f / 10-6

Curator: V. Voskresensky

IREzumi: Japanese Art of Tattoo

Japanese tattooists occupy a unique place in modern tattooing, blending traditional with contemporary themes. They have adapted Western colours and techniques to develop a style which is both distinctive and beautiful. Perhaps more than any other nationality they have brought art to tattooing, enriching both their own repertoire and that of tattooists in other countries who employ Japanese motifs in their own work.

Despite the popularity of the tattooing world wide, within the minds of most people, tattooing is most strongly associated on a national basis with Japan. Perhaps this is because it is within that country most unified, mostly densely applied, most finely detailed and most completely covering tattoos are found - for certainly the incidence of tattooing is not markedly greater there than any other country. Further, within Japan there is a certain air of mystery associated with tattoos, an ambience not found elsewhere. This air of mystery complements the Western notions of the 'exotic Orient'.

To the Japanese, tattoos are the art of the Ire-zumi, literally meaning the 'insertion of ink'. or more classically and elegantly *hori-mono*, meaning something which is 'carved', 'sculpted' or 'engraved'. The word most commonly used is contracted to *Irezumi*, and it may be used either as an adjective or a noun, and applied either to the tattooist, the wearer of a tattoo or to the inked design itself, indeed it may even refer to that group of people who are involved in tattoo art.

Within Japan today, there are perhaps a hundred recognised practitioners of Irezumi and perhaps 75,000 to 100,000 wearers of tattoos. In a densely populated country of 127 million people, that is a small proportion of people

indeed, yet the mystery associated with Irezumi remains, and continues to impress. So much so, that the practice of Irezumi is recognised both a legitimate art and the mark of the Yakuza, a criminal element of Japanese society.

Tattooing was known in ancient Japan, but it was very far from an art form then. In the second of Japan's two earliest historical records, *Nihongi*, compiled in AD 720, a brief mention is made of an emperor who commuted his cook's death sentence to a life-long sentence of ostracism by means of 'facial tattoo'. Tattoos continued to be used to stigmatise wrongdoers up until the eighteenth century.

It was in that century, during the Edo period, that tattooing began to flourish. The Edo period was a time of social upheaval, with the common people seething with resentment towards the largely hereditary and socially elite warrior caste. During this period, the basis of the Japanese economy changed from rice to gold and reforms were instituted whereby, although still socially oppressed, the common people were granted the right to seek pleasures. Soon, merchants began to surpass the somewhat austere but ruling samurai in material terms – particularly in their extravagant displays of wealth.

Together with the willow world of the geishas, literature, puppet theatre and other recreational pursuits, licensed

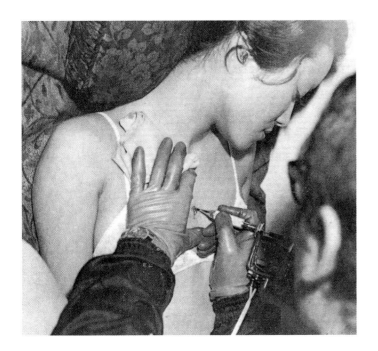

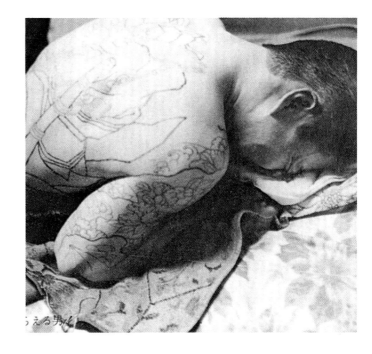

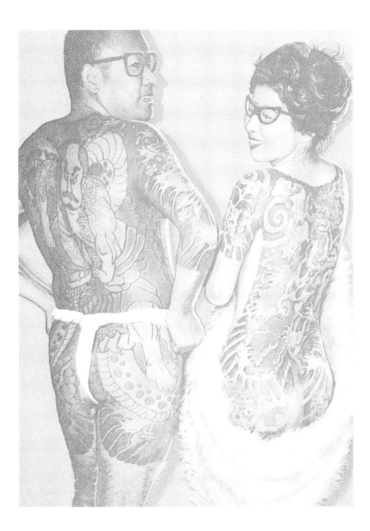

premises and bathhouses began to flourish - and tattooing came very strongly in to vogue. Courtesans tattooed themselves with 'promise engravings' known as *kisho bori*, erotic or evocative phrases linked into hidden parts of their bodies and visible only when naked or in the act of love-making. Many of the men tattooed themselves more visibly, some quite prominently, as part of the bluster of being recognised as 'chivalrous commoners'. Popular picture prints of the day, now highly prized by art connoisseurs, clearly document both the variety and prevalence of the tattoos of those times.

In 1805, an event occurred which was both of considerable importance to both Japanese culture generally, and to the evolution of Irezumi in particular. This was the publication of Bakin's translation of a fourteenth century Chinese series of stories based in historical fact. Bakin, a novelist, entitled the work *Suikoden* - which translates as the 'Water's Margin' or in the Sino-English of Pearl Buck 'All Men Are Brothers'. It is a series of tales of heroic deeds performed by Sung Chiang and his roving band of *hoa han* bravos, or 'men to be feared'. This swashbuckling group, many noted as being tattooed, were roughly a parallel to the legend of Robin Hood: forcibly retrieving the ill-gotten riches accumulated by corrupt officials. Despite their ferocious savagery they righted wrongs, protected the weak, and respected children and the aged. To beg forgiveness, they bared their tattooed backs to be beaten.

The effect of the *Suikoden* on Japan was immediate and galvanizing. The commoners suddenly had a number of

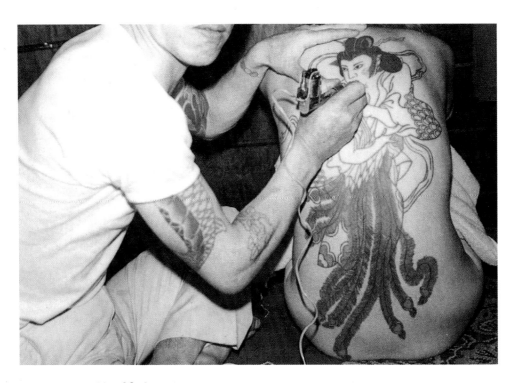

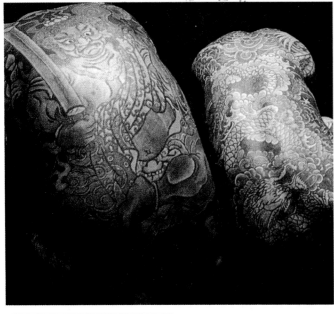

Many Japanese tattoos are large pieces which are integrated into an overall design, with full back tattoos being relatively common.

'heroes' quite unrelated to the ruling class of the samurai and they took to them with great gusto. The Japanese kabuki theatre adapted the tales into plays and artists illustrated them. One noted artist, Kuniyoshi, became an instant sensation with his series of pictures entitled '108 Heroes of *Suikoden'*. Bakin's book and Kuniyoshi's prints set the fashion for, and established the canons of the art of tattooing, tenets which are still followed in the compositions of present-day Irezumi.

The vogue for tattoos in Japan came to an abrupt halt in the 1850s. Until that time, contact with Europeans had been strictly limited, and Japan remained a feudal nation which was closed to the rest of the world. At that time the European powers began seeking access to Japan, and with the arrival of an American fleet commanded by Admiral Matthew Perry in 1853, Japan was forced to grant that access.

Forced to open itself to foreign scrutiny, Japan became acutely sensitive to the opinions and tastes of the technologically superior nations. Since virtually none of the Europeans were tattooed, the formerly popular tattooing pursuits came to be considered 'common'. So acute was the national embarrassment of the Japanese, and so fearful were the ruling classes of appearing barbarous to Western eyes or rendering Japanese culture contemptible to the foreigners, that tattooing was summarily interdicted in 1869. Police raided the mansions and studios of tattoo masters, and confiscated or destroyed all of the paraphernalia of their

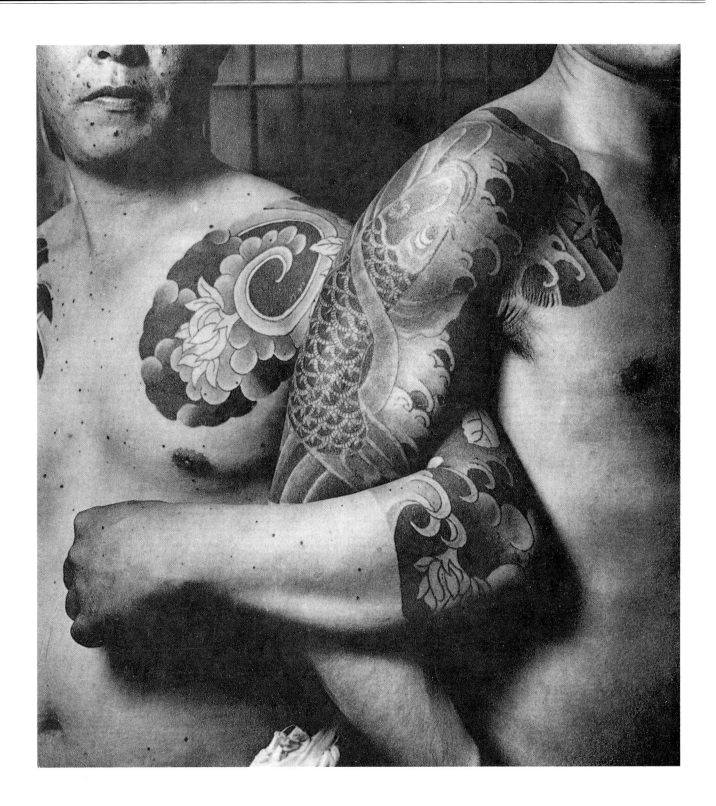

三代目
彫よし

By Horiyoshi II

calling. Although the seeds of the Irezumi were already planted, the prevalence and popularity of tattooing never regained its former prominence.

Soon a baffled administration realised it may have been over-zealous: many of the foreign embassies actively sought the most completely tattooed coolies as their rickshaw pullers - but the interdiction had exerted the desired effect and the damage was already done. Officials compromised: noted tattoo master Horicho was permitted to establish a studio in the port city of Yokohama, but was obliged to erect a sign reading 'For Foreigners Only'. It was to this studio that two young midshipmen, on naval tours, were to come to have dragons tattooed on their forearms. One was an English prince (later to become King George V) and one a Russian tsarevich (later to become Tsar Nicholas II). An opportunity to 'export' the service to the foreigners had been destroyed.

By the nineteenth century, tattooing had slowly recovered to a point where trade guilds of *horoshi* (tattoo experts) had formed, but they were still of the lower caste. They were street artisans and barbers who catered to the 'naked trades': coolies, porters, gardeners, palanquin bearers, rickshaw pullers, and others whose work forced them to strip down to near nudity. The often flamboyant tattoos these people wore, although individual, tended to classify and stratify the labours they represented, and as social attitudes changed, these marking became to be considered shameful. The art of Irezumi, still based in the classical tales of the *Suikoden*, was forced to become an'underground; and 'fringe' activity. It still is.

Most of the people who are heavily tattooed live encased and enclosed in the special and rather isolated world of Irezumi, a realm noted as being very clannish and difficult to penetrate. They form a *nakama*, or close-knit group of companions: self-contained, shielded from outsiders, aware of their difference and bound together by a defiant sense of outcast camaraderie. Few claim any intimate friends, but they will boast of the cohesion and self-sufficiency of their nakama. At the centre of the nakama is the Irezumi practitioner, for loyalty is strong, and few Irezumi devotees would ever contemplate being tattooed by anybody outside their own clique. Further, only one Irezumi master is capable of completing a large design once it is underway. His work is so individual that it is instantly recognisable to other practitioners - so much so that Irezumi work is occasionally used by Japanese police in the identification of unknown corpses. Despite the closed nature of the nakama, the Irezumi master's life is always intensely competitive: he must continue to develop his art, extend his repertoire and clientele - and there is always the fear that another practitioner of the art may copy a secret colour, pattern or needle technique.

A curious relationship develops between the practitioner and his subject, and this is always respected. The master does not advertise and is not listed in the telephone books.

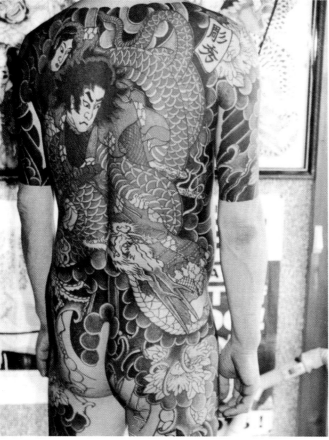

His fame rests only on word of mouth, but members of the nakama will not reveal his identity or address without the group's tacit consent. He will tattoo nobody unless he feels some empathy with them, regardless of the sum of money that may be offered. Conversely he will tattoo free of charge for somebody who particularly pleases him. Many days will be spent with a client discussing a tattoo before a needle touches the flesh: pattern, placement, purpose and desire are considered to be vitally important.

Among some nakamas there may be a covert element of homosexuality, but this is a taboo subject and never openly discussed. More damaging to the art of Irezumi than this, has been its putative association with the *Yakuza*, a criminal element of Japanese society. The Yakazu is constituted of some two thousand criminal organisations with an estimated membership of one hundred thousand people, and it is heavily involved in prostitution, pornography, extortion and drug dealing. Japanese police estimate the overall Yakuza income to be in the order of five billion dollars annually. About sixty to seventy percent of Yakuza members adorn themselves with tattoos for much the same reasons as law-abiding Irezumi: they pride themselves on being identifiable as members of an outcast and worthless social group. Consequently, the spread of the art of the Irezumi has suffered from a common fear among Japanese citizens that if they are tattooed they may be mistaken for a Yakuza criminal.

Who then are the Irezumi? Why are they so heavily tattooed and what is so special about their Irezumi tattoos? The subjects are most often men: generally outwardly gentle, often lonely, eager to meet and impress women but frequently shy and insecure. The nakama seems to fill the role of family for many of them, and the tattoo to act as a shield against the outside world. Even those Irezumi rumoured to be connected to the Yakuza tend to be quiet and courtly. Few are married. If a tattooed man marries, it tends to be to a woman who is attracted as much to the power and strangeness of the tattoo as the same qualities in the man himself, and such women then often become Irezumi themselves. Generally, normal women are not attracted to tattooed men, although myth holds that Irezumi are attractive and no woman ever refuses them.

The reasons behind becoming an Irezumi are both complex and obscure. It is generally agreed that tattooing increases the good life, but substantiation of this claim is virtually impossible to find. Certainly, there are few advantages to compensate for the disadvantages. To complete a full-body tattoo costs thousands upon thousands of yen and may demand anywhere between two and ten years. The pain suffered in its completion is excruciating, despite the lacing of some inks with cocaine, and it has the effect of shortening lifespan, since too little skin is left free to perspire and 'breathe'. Certain coloured inks, notably red may contain poisonous elements such as cadmium which pose serious

Japan's tattoo enthusiasts may be a minority movement in the country, but they make up for it in sheer colour and excitement, as both men and women appreciate the drama of large bold designs.

health risks if applied too liberally. Further, because the strong social stigmatisation still remains, Irezumi must dress carefully to conceal their bodily decorations.

The Irezumi are undoubtedly as subject to self-love and narcissism as anybody else, but Irezumi is more than an expression of this alone. Part of the attraction of tattooing undoubtedly lies in its defiant isolation of the individual from the norm of society, coupled with a strong sense of group identity, but there is also the spiritual side. Most Irezumi illustrations are designed around the tenets of the *Suikoden* or inspired by kabuki plays, and tend to glorify spiritual values such as patience, courage, perserverance, generosity and loyalty. Naturally, such designs are highly personal and individualised.

Technically, Irezumi are in a class alone. Japanese Irezumi practitioners usually use both modern electronic tattooing machines and also traditional bamboo and steel needles of varying fineness. Their work is characterised not only by the spiritual values of their designs but also by large unified swirling compositions, deep perspective, delicately refined detail and gradual shadings. The finest areas, such as highlights and accents. are applied using *hanebari*, a fluttering technique where the needles feather in myriad minute punctures. This technique is found only in Japan.

Irezumi designs may be large or small, but because of the combination of time, pain and cost that is involved, full body tattoos remain rare. Horikin, a leading contemporary Irezumi master, estimates that only one per cent of those who ask for a full body tattoo actually accomplish their aim, and of the roughly two thousand Japanese with half body tattoos, only about two hundred will see them through to full body status. Of course, not all Irezumi seek a full-body tattoo, for it does have practical disadvantages. Some seek half body tattoos or even just a sleeve or chest design. Others may ask for a one-fourth body tattoo, which are usually executed in the 'river' style. This style is designed to leave gaps of untouched flesh strategically placed so that the tattoo may be hidden even when wearing the traditional casual outfit of happi coat and calf length mompei trousers.

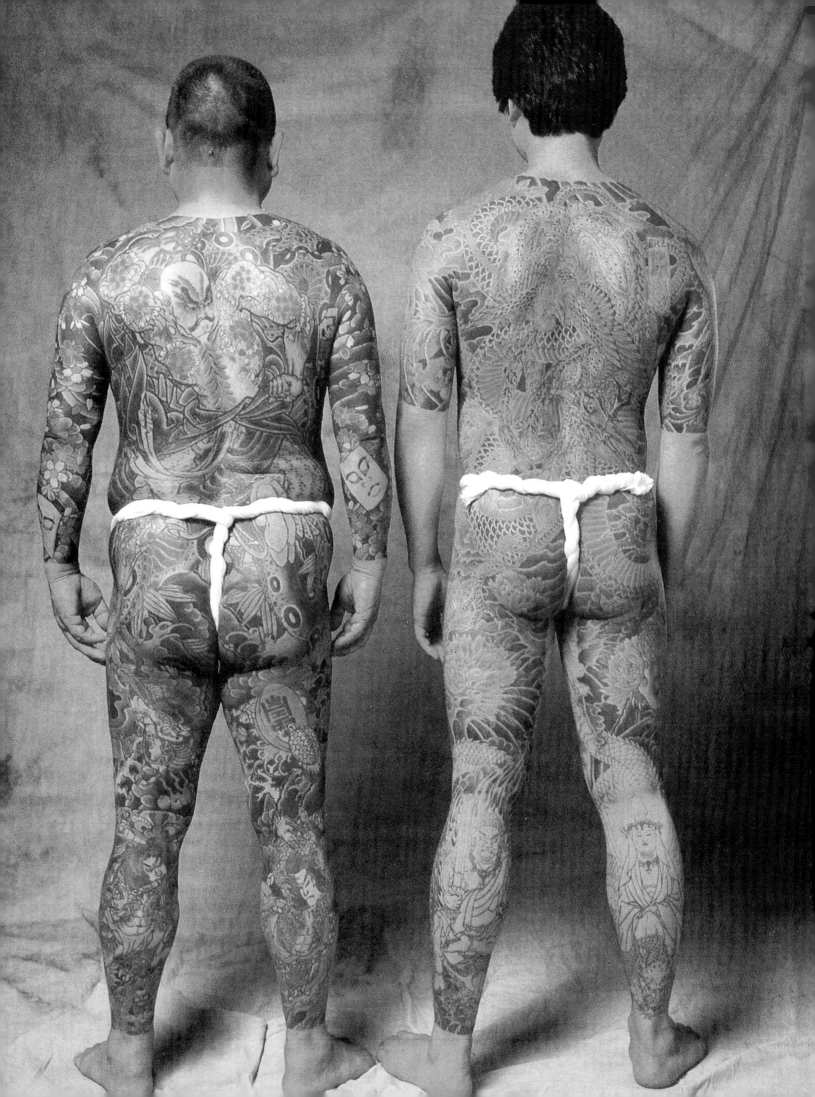

Artist's portrayal of a Suikoden hero. Toyokuni. Mid-1800's.

Japanese Flash

Japanese tattoo designs have been influenced by mainstream Japanese art and many tattoos are derived from wood-cut prints produced by artists of the eighteenth and nineteenth century. Some of these prints were made to illustrate famous stories from Japanese and Chinese literature, folk tales and mythology. Traditional Japanese tattoos are imbued with meaning and often tell a story.

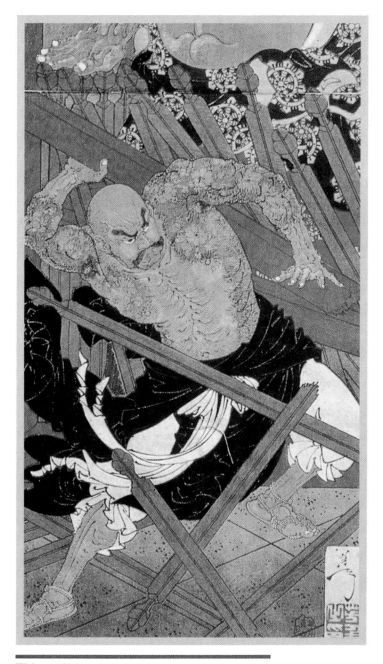

This traditional design features Roshishin the mad monk. He is brandishing an iron staff.

From a print by Yoshitoshi. His skill and fine workmanship has made him one of the great inspirations for tattoo artists.

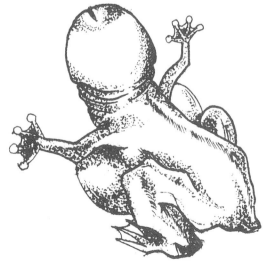

Japanese art generally and tattoo art in particular, has always had strong erotic elements, but some modern Japanese tattoo artists are much more explicit and are exploring all elements of sexual activity including sadomasochism. The designs on these pages are by Kazuo Oguri.

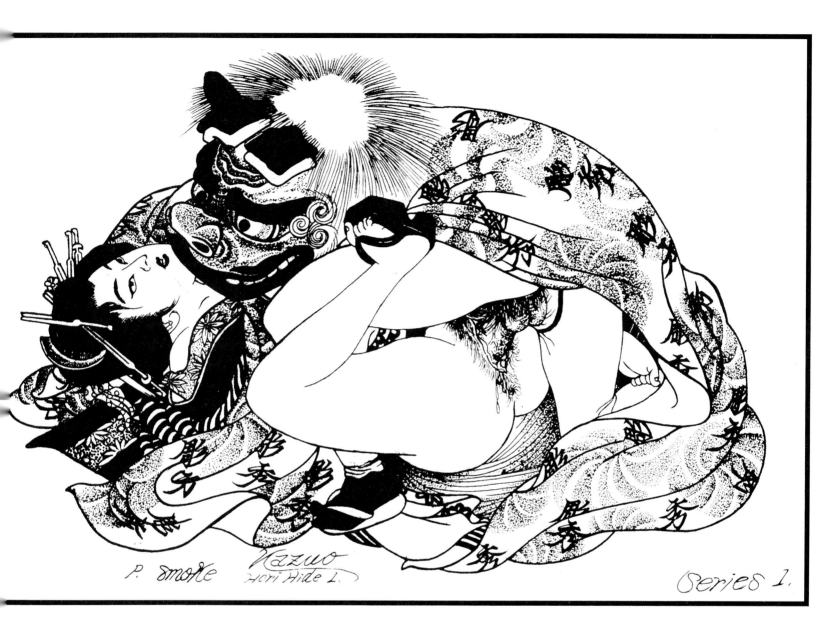

P. Smoke   Kazuo Hori Hide I.   Series 1.

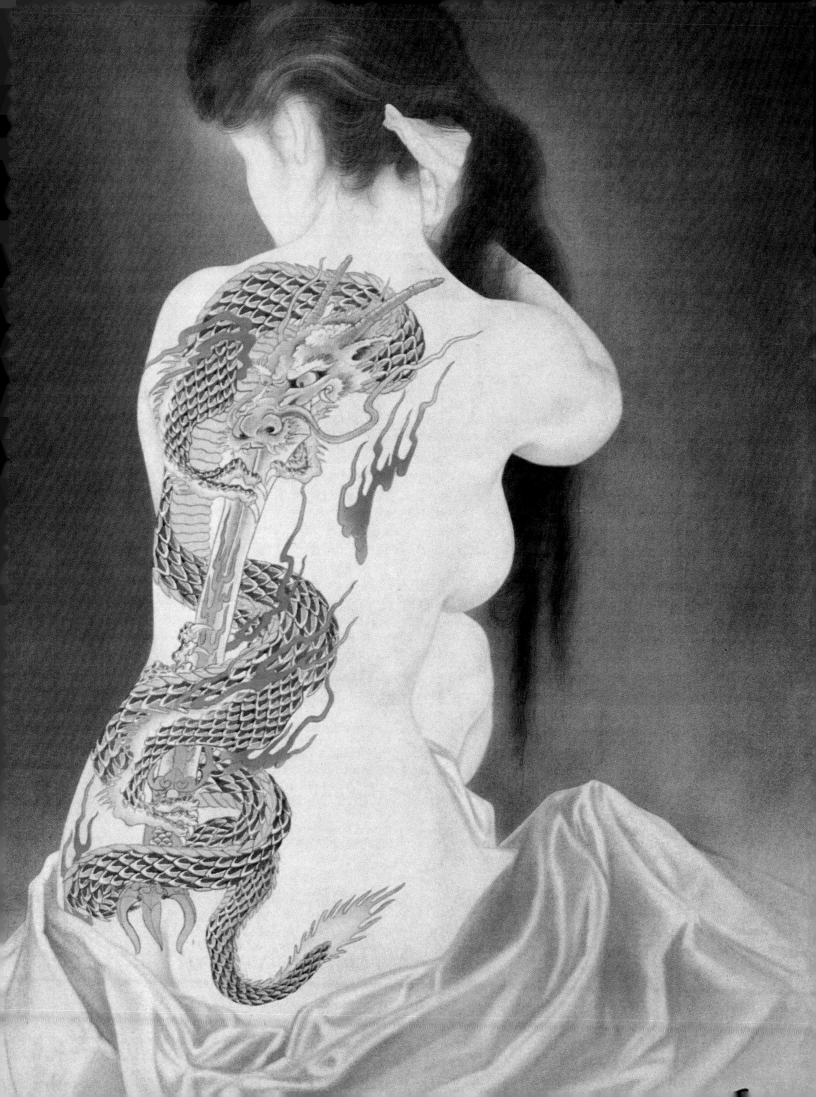

(Above) Wally Hammond, a long time Sydney tatttoist photographed at the Red Light Studio in 1982.

(Left) Doc Forbes, a "Famous Tattoo Artist" to quote his card, with Donna. His card also carried the legend - "Marry a fat tattooed lady and you'll get heat in the winter shade in the summer and moving pictures all year round."

The Tattooists

Tattooists today owe a great deal to those that have gone before and in conversations with tattoo artists the same names keep cropping up – Bob Shaw, Les Skuse, Sailor Jerry, Cliff Raven, Lyle Tuttle, Wally Hammond, Bert Grimm, George Burchett, Percy Walters, Kazuo Oguri – and as most of them are tattooed themselves, this section is dedicated to these craftsmen with pictures from the Cohen Collection.

Bob Shaw, one of the most influential American tattoo artists, after his discharge from the army in 1946. These tattoos were by Bert Grimm.

Hanky Panky and Kazuo Oguri taken in Gifu City, Japan. (Below) Alex Chater, Paddington, Sydney.

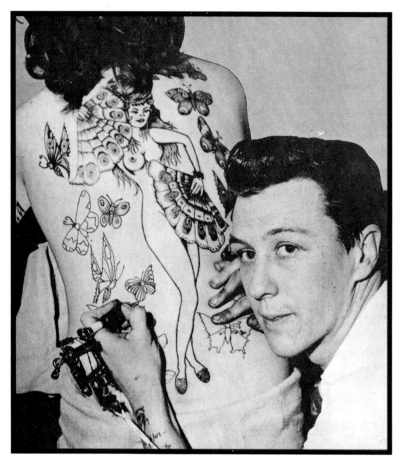

Famous British tattoo artist, Terry Wrigloy.

(Above)The tattooing of Cindy Ray is one of the most well documented tattooing events in Australia. Practically every session, with a number of different tattooists was carefully photographed. The man doing the work in this photograph is Les Bowen.

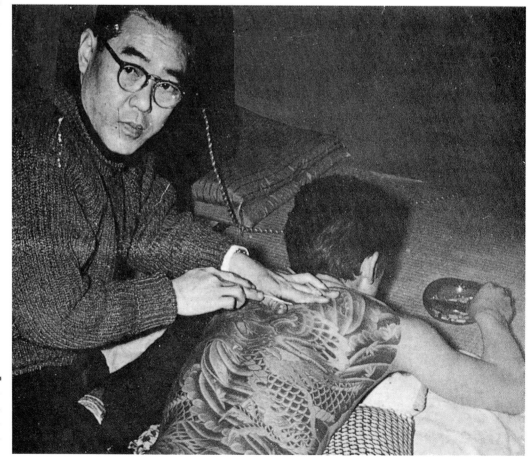

(Right) Japan's most famous tattoo artist, Horioshi II, at work with traditional equipment.

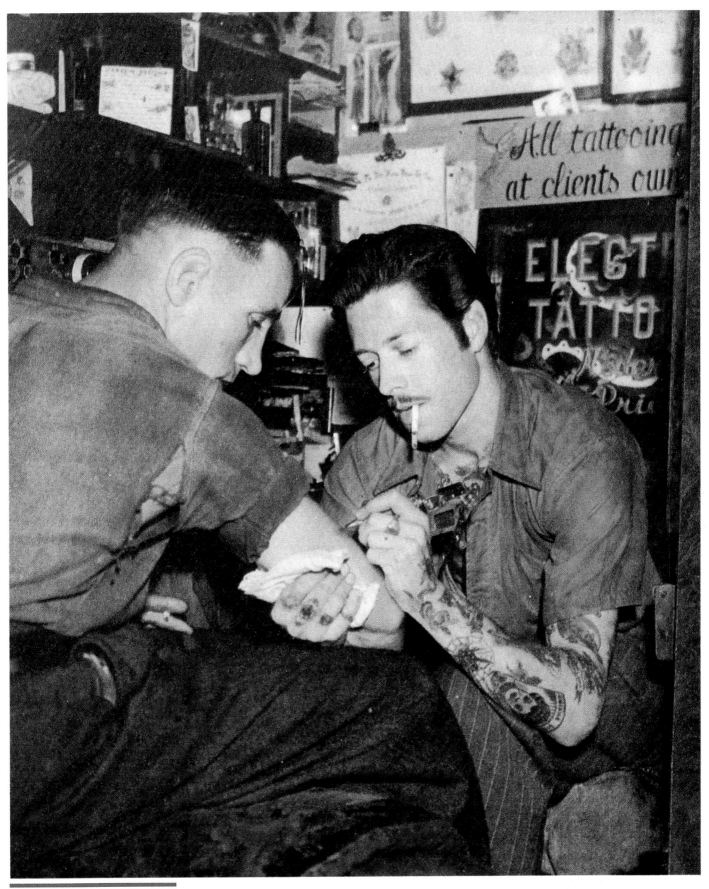

"The Lone Wolf" – Inky
Horsler of Luton, England.

(Above) Lyle Tuttle – Ever the showman, every picture of Lyle shows his flair and style. (Bottom) Les Skuse. 1973. (Top right) Bill Phillips, Eddie Funk and Tony Cohen. (Bottom right) Tony with Horioshi III.

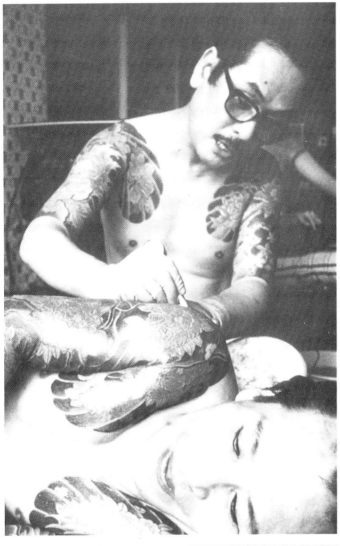

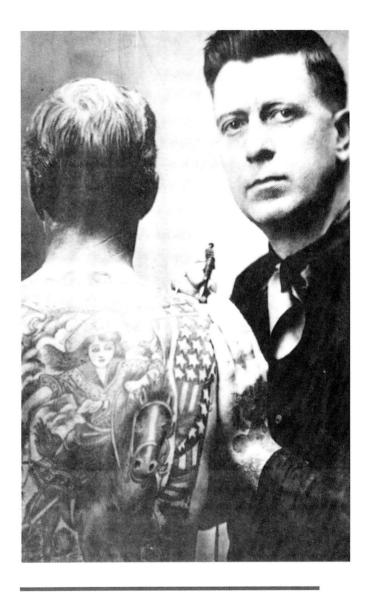

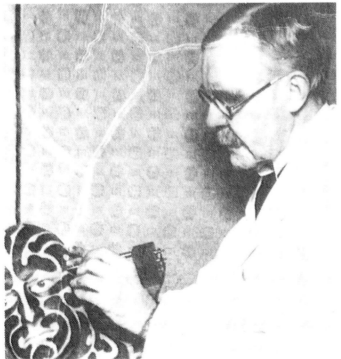

(Top left) Horioshi, one of the most renowned of the traditional Japanese tattoo artists at work. (Top Right) Ben Corday, although an Englishman did most of his work in the United States. (Left) George Burchett, one of Britain's most famous tattooists at work on his most famous client - Omi.
(Below) George's wife Edith "My best model".

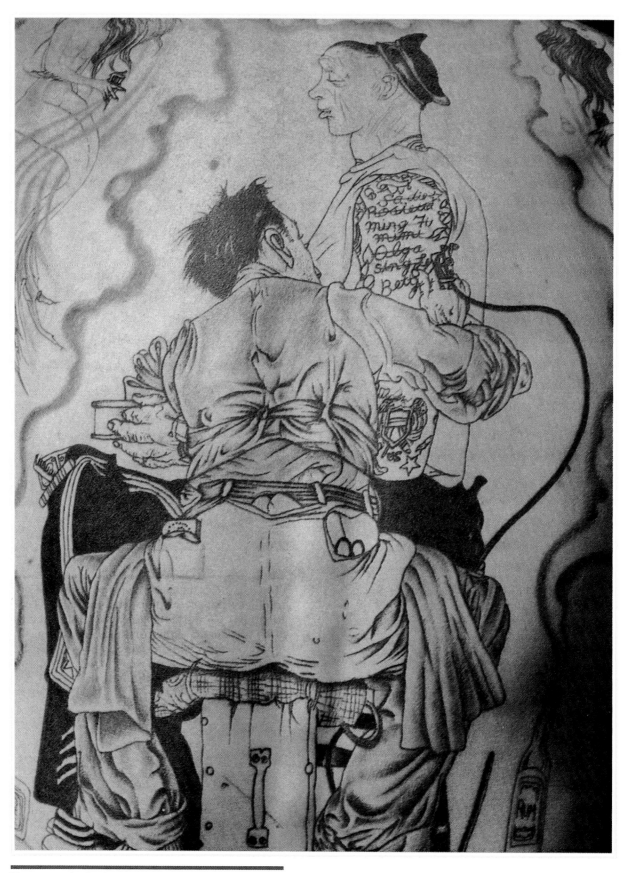

Tattoo on Andy Capp U.S.A. after a painting by famous American painter Norman Rockwell.

WHAT IS A TATTOOIST?

IN A BACK STREET GROT, one might find a magical character, known as the TATTOOIST.
He comes in many shapes, sizes and nationalities,
Fat, thin, cosmopolitan and miscellaneous.
He is Truth, with a Professor's know-how and black ink under his nails,
Beauty, with a tailored, splattered off-white jacket
And the hopes of all artisans, with your arm in his blood-stained claws...
He can be discovered, caught or found - sometimes,
On top of, sliding from, creeping past or disrobing
Anything that is female, semi-nude or alcoholic.
He likes beer by the quart, naked virgin flesh - preferably maidens,
TATTOOED hooligans, his bed and fistfuls of fivers...
He cares not for credit, Boy Soldiers, Non-tippers and his own cigarettes.
Nobody is so slow to rise yet so quick to make a quid.
When authorities object, he protests with his only weapon, BULLSHIT
When you're nervous, he's an inconsiderate, sadistic, grinning bastard.
When you're a roughie toughie hard-case, covered in boot polish TATTOOS,
He just sits there, like a Mafia godfather, sneers prettily and adds ten per cent...
NO one else can cram in his skull, the winners of yesterday's race meetings,
A dead cert cure for gangrene, the entire Criminal Law, the sickest of jokes,
And the medical properties of the potion he's just slopped on your arm.
Under his table, he can cram a clapped-out battery, a filthy sex book,
A jar of painkillers (at ten bob each), packet of three,
A wad of blue photos, six broken watches, pictures of the KING OF DENMARK,
And the local Rat-Bag with TATTOOED tits...
BIKERS love him, Mothers hate him, his bird just tolerates him,
The neighbours ignore him and his tall stories protect him.
But he'll baffle you with science, tales of poverty, produce his Guild and Club certificates
And have you heading for the Labour Exchange, after smoking your last fag...
LET'S FACE IT
He'll TATTOO your bird, the vicar's daughter, a queer's posterior
Or you old Granny's varicosed boobs.
He'll smoke all your fags, take you last quid, drink your last ale
Then expect a tip - all with a smile on his ink-splashed face.
He'll take your prized possessions, your dole money,
And your sweetheart for his works of art - but no tick!
He's your mate, confident, champion of the lost and luckless,
A hard drinking, conniving opponent of Back Alley Scratchers,
A man alone, the poor man's Rembrandt - the TATTOOIST...
But when you crawl into his shop after a day of boozing it up,
Having been filled in, spewed on and hen-pecked,
With all you hopes for the future lying shattered and ruined,
And on return have to defraud the Railways and explain the TATTOOS
He'll mend them all like new with his latest design and a few words:
WHATTO SCABBY! Sit down and relax and pass them fags.

From the pen of Painless Jeff Baker, long time tattooist and old friend of Tony Cohen's of Deal, Kent, England.

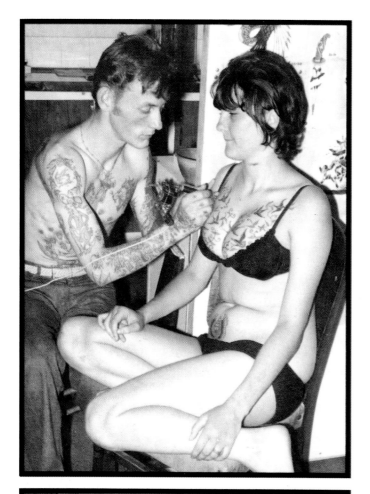

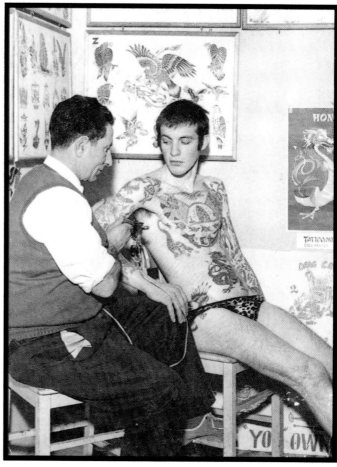

(Top left) Ross McAlpine of
Melbourne, Victoria.
(Above) Bev and Danny
Robinson and (left) Bob
Shaw tattooed by Bert
Grimm .

Tony Cohen. June, 1994.

Bev Robinson at work.

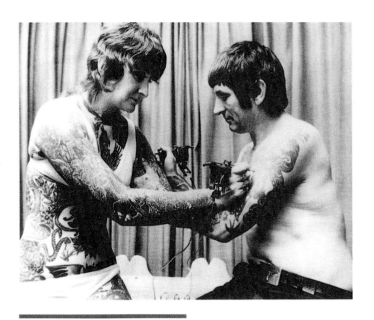

Is this a good idea? Bill and
Rusty Skuse.

There's no doubt about it. A
tattooist knows how to offer
a bargain.

A WARM WELCOME from A RED·HOT·ARTIST
-He forgot to give me a fag!
Come·up·and·see·me·sometime---
Thousands·have, for·over·25 YRS.

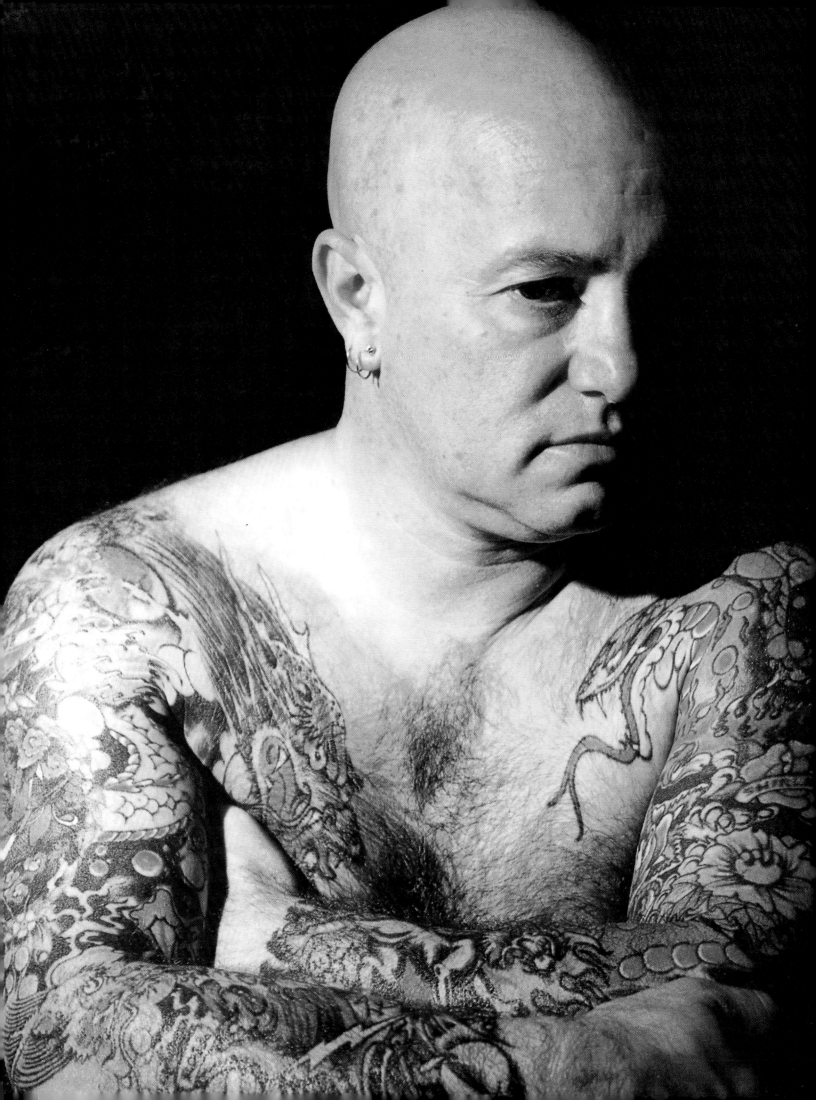

Tattoo Australia

The resurgence of European interest in tattooing, a practice which had been virtually dead on the European continent since the dark ages, began with Captain James Cook's voyages in the Pacific region in the eighteenth century. History tells us that Cook discovered Australia's eastern seaboard in 1770, and a mere eight years later. the British government founded a penal settlement, not at Botany Bay as planned, but at Sydney Cove on Port Jackson. Considering the short time span between the 'rediscovery' of tattooing and the European settlement of Australia, it is just possible, although not at all probable, that some of the first convicts and their guards may have been tattooed. History has not recorded whether this was so, but the likelihood of tattooed people being present among the first arrivals is extremely low.

Cindy Ray (Bev Robinson) was one of Australian tattooing's most tireless advocates in the 1960's, appearing in countless magazine articles promoting both tattooing generally, and also self-promoting her art.

While tattooing is alive and well in Australia, most of the designs follow traditional motifs from America, Europe and Japan. Until recently few tattooists have experimented with purely Australian-inspired designs. With the advent of specialist magazines more thought is being given to Australian themes in tattooing. This doesn't mean that we should become all nationalistic and tattoo only kangaroos and wombats. The Australian mythology, both aboriginal and European, offers plenty of scope for inspiration. Ned Kelly is an obvious subject and one that has been given some attention already...

Despite this, the advent of tattooing in Australia apparently caused no historical ripple worthy of recording, even though the emergence of tattooing in Australia is much the same as in Europe and America, where ample historical records relating to the tattoos are found. It is interesting to speculate why this was so, particularly when Australians of European origin were in those days isolated by enormous distances and slow communications, and something as striking as tattooing could have been expected to provoke comment.

The lack of public comment about tattooing makes it not unreasonable to assume that Australians in the late nineteenth century had acquired a set of attitudes towards permanent bodily decoration which enabled them to accept tattooing without undue surprise, and that tattooing was slowly absorbed in Australia rather than suddenly becoming a notable and fashionable fad as it did in Britain. A number of diverse factors could have contributed to this predisposition or 'mind-set', including the Aborigines, the Maoris, and Polynesian 'kanakas', Japanese pearl divers, upper class British immigrants, and the many hundreds of seamen aboard vessels which sailed southwards to visit Australian ports.

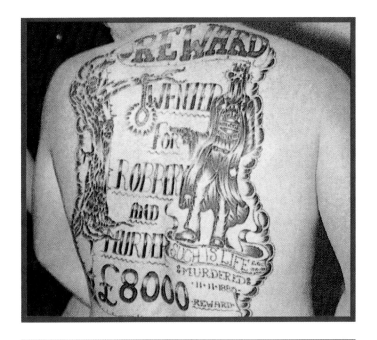

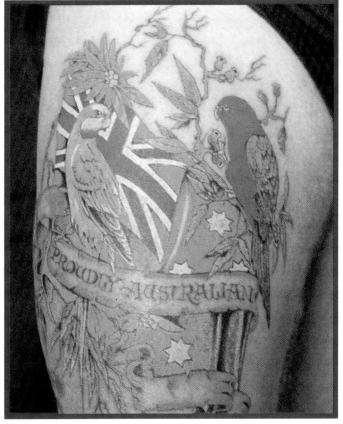

This selection of illustrations from *Australian Tattoo* magazine show that some tattooists are working with distinctly Australian themes. Tattoos by (Top left) Les Dent S.A, (Top Right) Rob Wilson, W.A. and (Above) Les Bowen, Townsville, Qld.

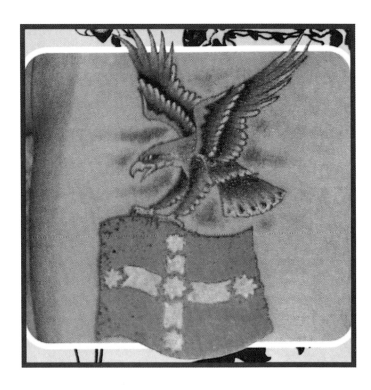

Australian fauna has potential as these birds from (Left) Peter Backman, Vic and (Right) Peter Davidson of Queensland illustrate. What's a bald eagle got that a wedgetail hasn't – except a bald head and a smaller wingspan?

The first of these influences was the presence of the Aborigines. The Aborigines, like most of the world's darker-skinned people were not a tattooed people, but they *did* practice cicatrisation: decorating their bodies with often quite prominent scars to mark membership of tribal clans or the passing of initiation rites. Thus the *idea* of direct bodily decoration was present in Australia, and readily observable, from the very earliest days.

The first direct contact early Australians probably had with tattooed people occurred in 1793, when the storeship *Daedalus* arrived in Port Jackson. Aboard her were two young Maori chiefs carried off from New Zealand to assist with the dressing of the flax which was being grown at Norfolk Island. Since the Maoris *were* a people renowned for tattooing, as that custom was particularly prevalent among the chieftains, it is not unreasonable to assume that these men were also tattooed, or at the very least, that the crew of the *Daedalus* had encountered tattooed people in the course of the two men's capture.

From that time onwards, there was some contact between Australia and New Zealand: five Maoris, a chief named Te Pehi accompanied by four of his sons, visited Sydney in 1806 where they were entertained by Governor King and the Reverend Samuel Marsden; a small but steadily growing maritime commerce began across the Tasman Sea with

some Maoris occasionally utilised as seamen; and by 1831 Governor Macquarie officially banned Australian participation in the trade in tattooed Maori heads. Further, the Maori wars of the 1860s excited a great deal of interest (albeit mainly antagonism) in the Maori people. Although Australians were yet to practise tattooing, many were undoubtedly acquainted with the idea of tattooing - and this was roughly three decades before the invention of the electric tattooing needle in America in 1891.

Those three decades brought an influx of other tattooed peoples into Australia, mainly to the remote north. The savage practice of 'blackbirding' - virtually a form of slavery - began in Queensland in the 1860s mainly to provide labour for the sugarcane fields. Unscrupulous seafarers were paid to raid many of the islands of the Pacific Ocean to bring back indentured labourers, who were kept at pathetic rates of pay in deplorable conditions and forced to labour for extensive periods before being repatriated to their homes - it they were sufficiently hardy and fortunate. The people captured, known by the derogative term 'kanakas' were of Polynesian, Micronesian and Macronesian origins - and many were undoubtedly tattooed since the practice of tattooing was commonplace in these cultures. Blackbirding was outlawed in 1890, began again briefly in modified form about the turn of the century, and then was

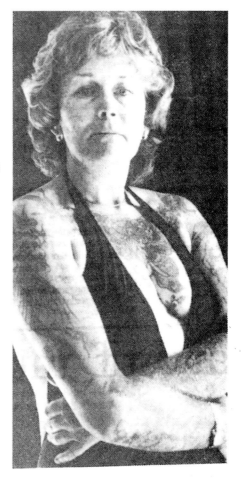

(Top left & Centre) Two
designs by Nutz, while the
portrait (Top right) is of
Bev Robinson, who was
Australia's best known
female tattoo artists in the
seventies and early eighties.
Kiwi Kim also worked with
The Illustrated Man before
opening her own studio.

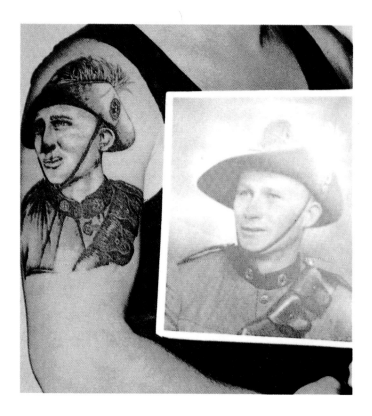

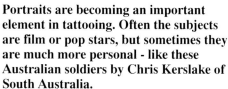

Portraits are becoming an important element in tattooing. Often the subjects are film or pop stars, but sometimes they are much more personal - like these Australian soldiers by Chris Kerslake of South Australia.

finally halted. Eventually, all of the Pacific Islanders were expelled from Australia, but their influence had lasted several decades and the memory of their tattoos was sure to have lingered.

Another significant influx of people from a tattoo conscious society began in 1876. In that year Nonami Kojuro, a seaman and the first Japanese citizen to arrive in Australia, signed off his ship in Sydney. He subsequently joined the crew of a pearling lugger and quite quickly distinguished himself as a pearl diver. Within a short time, hundreds of Japanese men has emulated him. Indeed, Japanese men came to be held in high esteem as divers, and quite large Japanese communities became established at Thursday Island and Broome, and remained until the outbreak of World War II. Among them were tattooed men, some who had arrived prior to 1890.

Following the invention of the electric tattooing needle in 1891, tattoos became much more commonplace, partly because the process was quicker and partly because it was relatively 'painless'. Two groups of people began arriving in Australia sporting the new body 'art' seamen who had acquired their tattoos in foreign ports and upper class British immigrants who had participated in the new and fashionable fad of tattooing which had swept London. Doubtless, both groups stirred some interest - the seamen through their

'macho' image, and the Englishmen because of the 'fashionability' and 'respectability' they bestowed on tattooing. Both groups were of European origin - and so tattoos could no longer be relegated in the public consciousness to being simply a 'peculiar' habit of 'heathen' races.

Considering the operation of all these factors, it is safe to assume that by the turn of the century, despite a stubborn condemnation of it by the more ardently religious sections of the community, tattooing was generally accepted in urban Australia - although it had not yet become a widespread phenomenon.

The two World Wars also boosted the public 'image' of tattoos. Thousands of servicemen went away to fight for their country, and when they returned many were wearing tattoos acquired while serving overseas. Since the community regarded these men as 'heroes', criticising them for the trivial matter of being tattooed was patently hypocritical. Further, since most tattooed Australian men had been servicemen and hence 'heroes', the younger generation tended to regard tattoos as being an outward manifestation of manliness, while the older section of the community came to regard them as simply another overseas influence adopted by a younger generation of international travellers. General acceptance of tattoos had finally come to Australia,

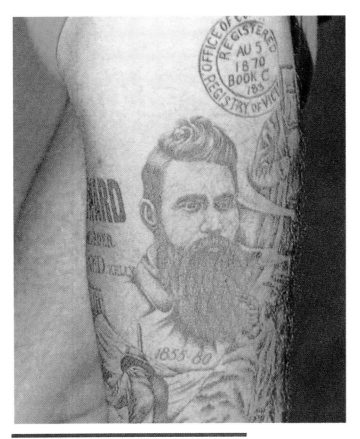

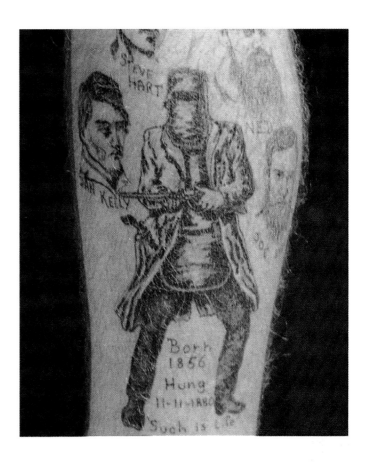

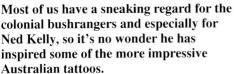

Most of us have a sneaking regard for the colonial bushrangers and especially for Ned Kelly, so it's no wonder he has inspired some of the more impressive Australian tattoos.

and it had arrived, without fuss or fanfare, over a very long period of gradual accustomisation.

Naturally, this period of accustomisation is reflected in the styles of tattoos seen on Australians of different generations. It should be remembered that prior to World War II, very few Australians travelled overseas because of the country's geographical isolation, because of limited personal opportunity, and because travel by sea was both slow and expensive. Hence, prior to World War I, tattoos were very rare. Those acquired overseas by servicemen during the period 1914-45 (from the beginning of World War I to the end of World War II) tended to be of common patterns found in the tattoo parlours of foreign ports or were generally of a military or patriotic nature. These tattoos tended to be relatively small and rather restricted in colouration.

The immediate postwar period saw a greater diversity of designs introduced: partly as a result of easier access to overseas destinations, and partly as a result of a more cosmopolitan attitude being introduced to Australia through massive immigration. The popular icons of a variety of cultures began to appear as tattoos. Later, as Australia experienced boom times, many people who had hitherto never dreamt of overseas travel found themselves flying off for overseas holidays - and with increasing frequency their destinations were Asian rather than European. Consequently, still more cultural icons of even greater diversity appeared as tattoos.

The past decade or so has seen the resurgence of interest in tattooing; not just within Australia, but world-wide. Many factors have a bearing on this global phenomenon: a greater and easier cultural crossflow, the introduction of a wider palette of colours in tattooing inks, a greater level of artistic appreciation and skill among tattooists, and importantly, a new set of less inhibited and more individual attitudes. This too, is reflected in the styles of tattoos now in vogue. Designs are more frequently large, colourful and better integrated than previously.

Within Australia, it is interesting to note that among the more universal themes used in tattooing, some distinctively Australian icons are already emerging. Often the work of tattooists such as Les Bowen, Colin Creed, Danny Robinson and some of the new breed of tattooists such as Fran Stintson, Nutz, Trevor McStay, Paul Braniff, Chris Reid and 'Kiwi' Kim, show Australian flora and fauna, or historic and folkloric emblems. Since national icons are often an important part of individual identity, the development of this style of work is a welcome addition to the repertoire of permanent body art.

Tattoo by Jack Rudy

AUSTRALIAN TATTOO GALLERY

Tony Cohen

The art of tattoo is as much knowing when to colour and when to leave skin bare, as it is of drawing. Fine tattoos are a harmonious blend of pigment and skin tone, delicate shading, and placement on the body, while the design and drawing create the initial impact. Like many other things these days, tattooing is subject to all sorts of international influences and most tattoos created in Australia reflect this with a wide range of subjects being chosen.

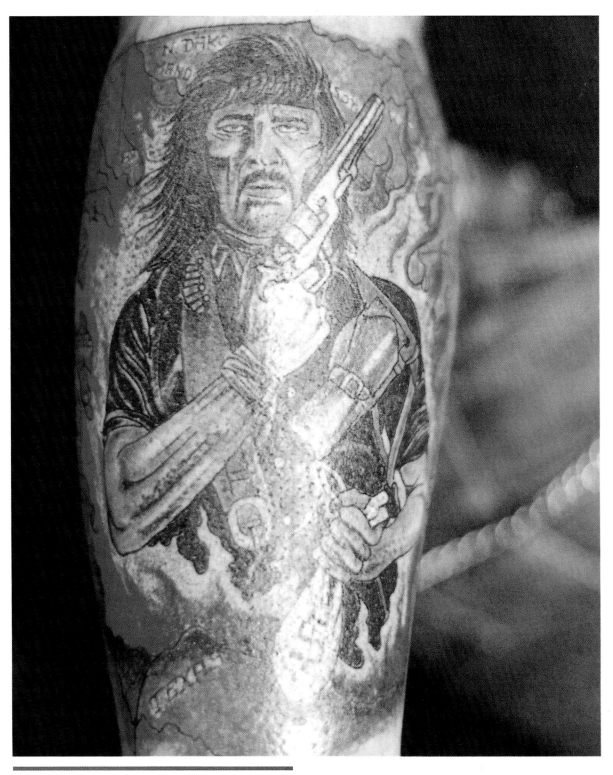

Andy Hicks tattooed by Tony Cohen.

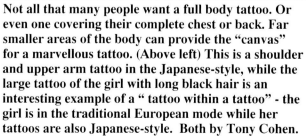

Not all that many people want a full body tattoo. Or
even one covering their complete chest or back. Far
smaller areas of the body can provide the "canvas"
for a marvellous tattoo. (Above left) This is a shoulder
and upper arm tattoo in the Japanese-style, while the
large tattoo of the girl with long black hair is an
interesting example of a " tattoo within a tattoo" - the
girl is in the traditional European mode while her
tattoos are also Japanese-style. Both by Tony Cohen.

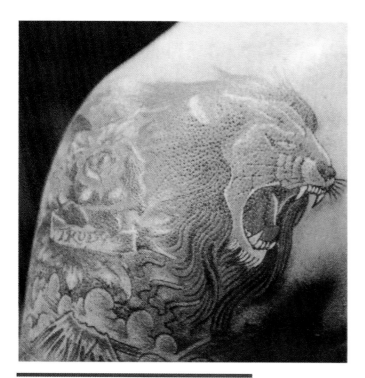

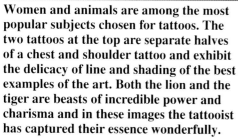

Women and animals are among the most popular subjects chosen for tattoos. The two tattoos at the top are separate halves of a chest and shoulder tattoo and exhibit the delicacy of line and shading of the best examples of the art. Both the lion and the tiger are beasts of incredible power and charisma and in these images the tattooist has captured their essence wonderfully.

Opposite page. Variations on a theme. Although the bear may be shots of the same tattoo at different stages.

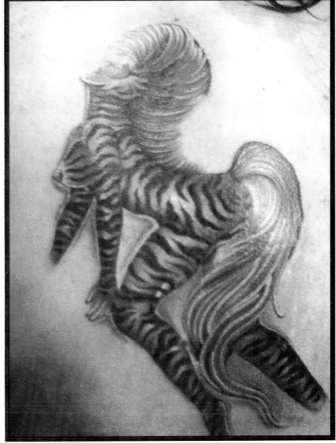

All tattoos by Tony Cohen.

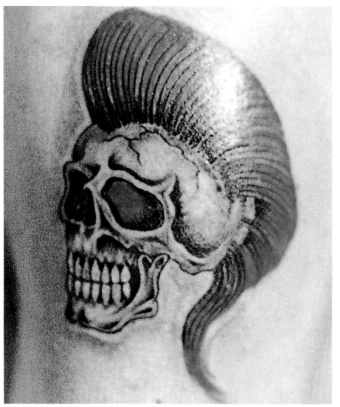

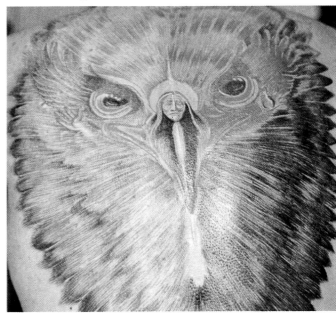

Probably because it offers the largest flat surface on the body the back is used to tattoo the most elaborate, detailed pictures. All of these large 'back-pieces' are astonishing examples of the tattooist's skill. (Top left) By Fran. (Top and bottom right) Tony Cohen and (bottom left) Rev John.

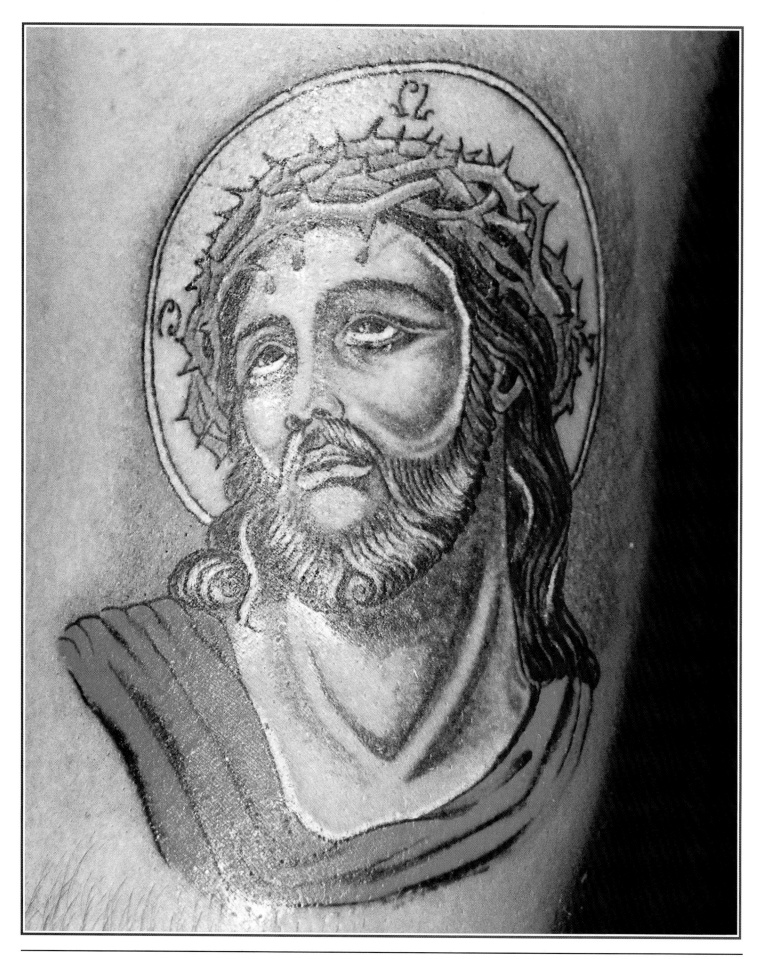

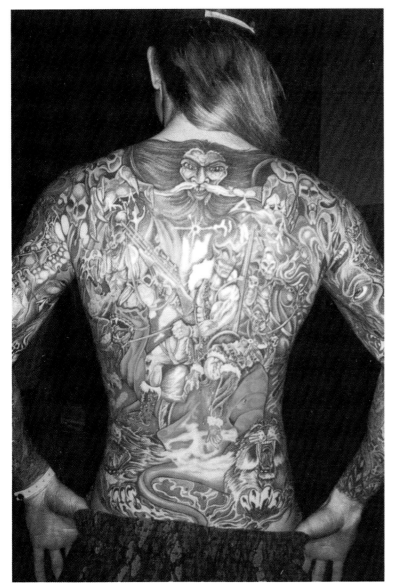

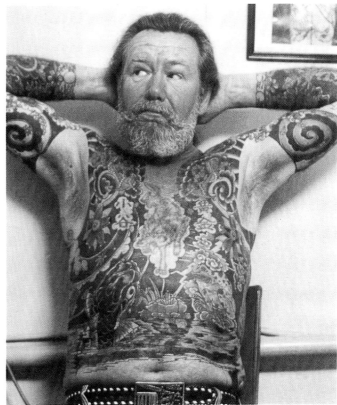

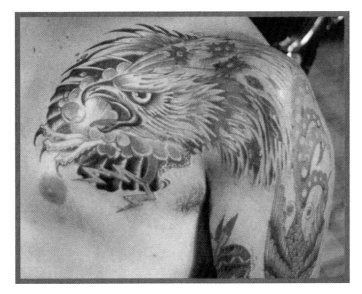

(Above) Glen Golden, Queensland tattooed by Pete Davidson. The others by Mario Bath on Bert Schreiner.

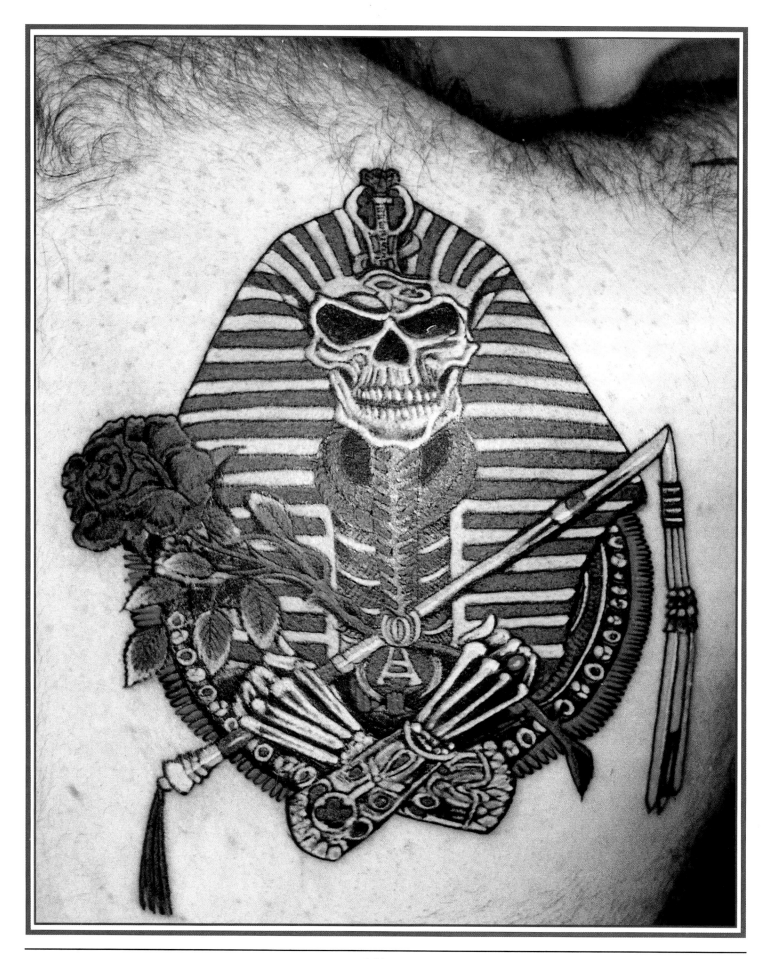

Danny Robinson and Tony Cohen

The tattoos on this double page illustrate the almost infinite variety of designs and variations on individual designs that are possible. While many tattoo designs are derived from 'flash' many more are completely original. Some creative abstract tattoos have been done, but the majority are of recognisable 'traditional' execution. That is not to say that tattooists and clients are unimaginative, but perhaps they do have a conservative streak.

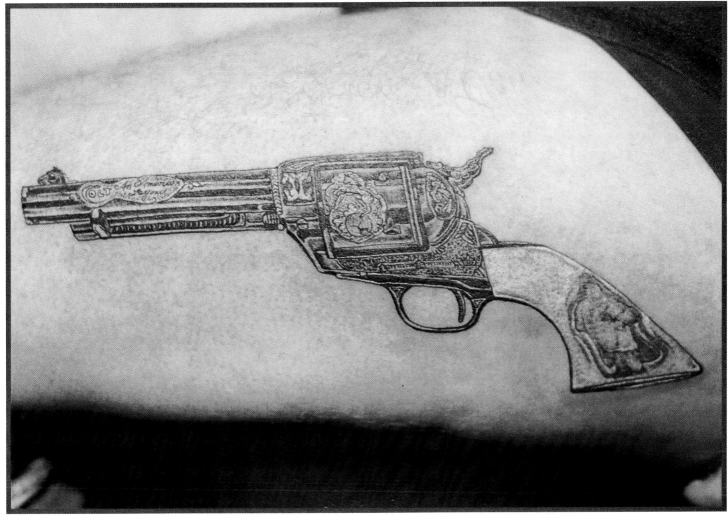

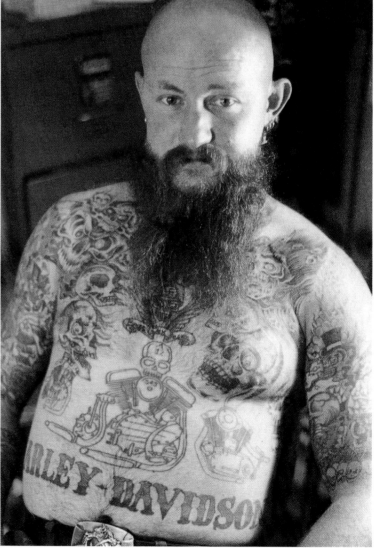

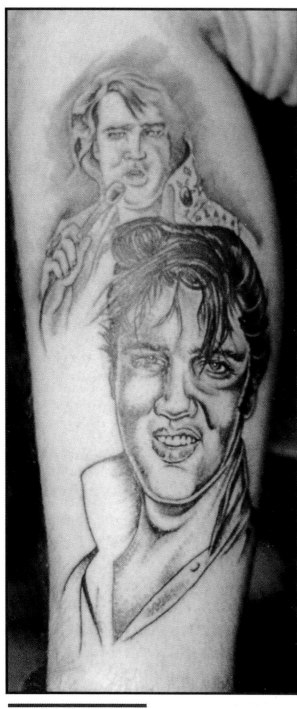

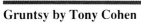

Gruntsy by Tony Cohen

A Bit Flash

While there are as many designs as there are tattooists - many thousands over the years - each artist has a selection of 'standard' tattoos. Prospective clients can look through this selection which is called flash to find one that suits. It probably won't come as a surprise to learn that there are specialist companies who supply flash for use by any tattooist who buys their designs.

Some flash is available in the forms of stencils allowing for fast application of the design, or giving less skilled operators, who are not good at drawing freehand, the chance to do first class work.

At one time proprietary flash could be poorly designed leading to poor execution of the tattoo, but much of the modern material is well drawn and interesting. However, the best is that designed and drawn by skilled practitioners and to whom the illustrations can almost be regarded as their trademarks.

Looking through any collection of flash it is obvious that there are a number of recurring themes: Harley Davidson motorcycle logos appear in variations never dreamed of by the factory, eagles, skulls, naked women, wizards and warlocks. There are monsters designed to give Frankenstein nightmares, as well as flowers, full-rigged sailing ships, snakes, bats, dragons and portraits of Elvis.

There are distinct differences between the subject matter of Western and, especially, Japanese tattoos although there are Western artists who work in the Japanese idiom.

Japanese tattoo artists draw extensively from their country's mythology, so their work makes uses of images of Samurai, golden carp, geishas, demons, lions, the Golden Boy, dragons and flowers.

Tattoos can depict extremes from the delicacy of an exquisitely rendered orchid, or a Celtic bracelet, to the violence of a raunchy S & M depiction of a naked woman trussed up like a chicken.

Flash reflects this range of material and is a good guide - maybe the best, since it is impossible to see all the work in the flesh - to the style and quality of a tattooist's work. Some have a portfolio of thousands of designs and a choice can be made from these - sometimes they are in the form of a photograph of a free-hand illustration done for a particular person. If the tattooist is honest these will remain unique designs, but there is nothing to stop other people from using them as a source of inspiration for their own tattoos.

All designs can be adapted, added to or subtracted from, elements of one combined with another, colours changed - that's one of the attractions of tattooing. Genuine individual designs are possible - it's up to the imagination!

Harley Davidsons have become an icon of popular culture and are one of the most tattooed devices. These are a selection from *The Illustrated Man's* collection.

The flash on the previous page and this page are typical of the older, simpler, less dynamic and more 'demure' style of tattooing and is directly descended from the work of the forties and fifties, interestingly, even in the late sixties the heart cost just $2.00, True Love $3.00.

Harley Davidsons, bikers and tattoos may be inextricably linked today, but modern tattooing began with sailors and ships. Even today many a studio is kept afloat by seamen – both navy and merchant marine. Almost every tattooists flash includes a number of nautical designs. Battleships may not be as popular as they were during World War 11, but fully-rigged sailing ships are as popular ever and are among the most spectacular of all tattoo designs. Which isn't surprising as they are, perhaps, the most graceful of man's machines. For as long as men and women, go down to the sea in ships they'll remain a part of every tattooists' library.

A Carp with Attitude... Tony Cohen's version of a traditional Japanese design. The carp is the King of the River Fish for eating. Myths surround the carp - one old Chinese tale tells of the carp that leapt up a waterfall and was turned into a dragon - another recurring image in tattooing.

**Birds of Prey – eagles and hawks – also
figure prominently in tattoo designs.**

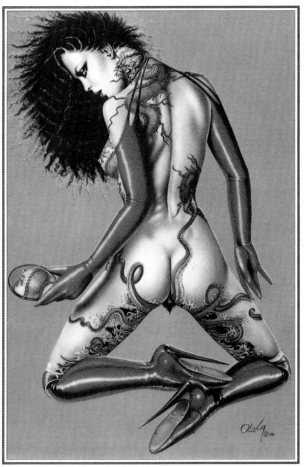

The comparison between the forties style of the girl and the rose and the modern design of 'Olivia' (left) is extraordinary.

Flash designs are varied owing much to influences as diverse as traditional Chinese art and the paintings of contemporary fantasy and science fiction illustrators. The subject matter is varied as the examples on these two pages show.

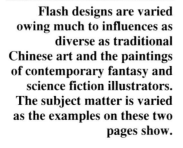

Painted Women

Tattooing started with women in ancient Eygpt over 4,000 years ago. In many cultures it is common in both men and women, but in Western society it was much more accepted for men than women. However, that is changing as more and more young women are becoming involved with tattoo art.

Tattoo artist Fran Stinson.

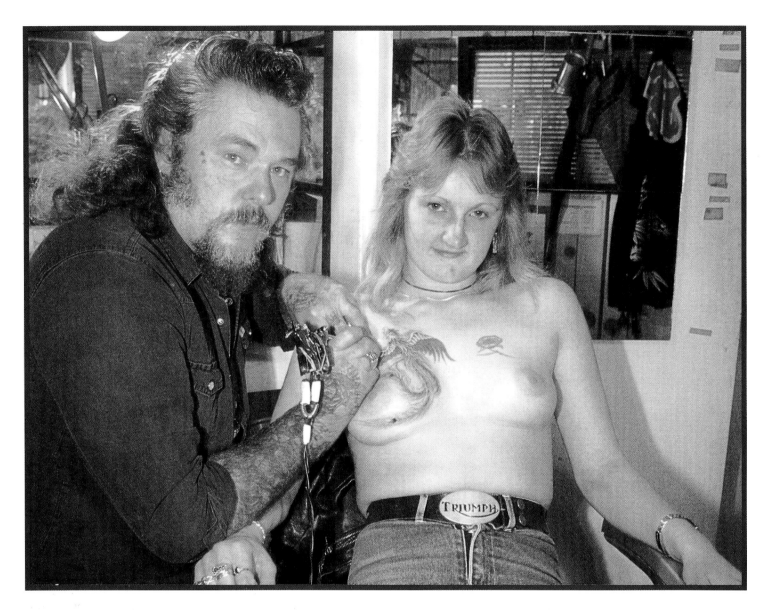

Tattooing is a very ancient craft, but because of religious influences, it became largely a lost art in European cultures until late in the eighteenth century, when it was 'rediscovered' as European ships penetrated ever further into the Pacific region and the New World of the Americas.

Until very recent times, at least among European peoples, tattooing was largely confined to menfolk, and the existence of a tattooed female was sufficiently rare and bizarre to excite a great deal of comment - usually very disparaging in nature. More than anything else, this is an illustration of the narrowness of traditional European attitudes, for tattooed ladies have always existed, just as tattooed men have, and in several non-European cultures their existence has often been a continuous and accepted cultural tradition. Nonetheless, the narrow European view of tattooed women was so strong that several otherwise normal women were exhibited in circuses or freak shows. They were gaped at by incredulous spectators, were advertised as rare curiosities

and were even subjected to 'scientific' examination by the 'intelligentsia' of their times.

Because tattooed women are relatively unremarkable today, yet created something of a furore in the past, the subject merits comment. Quite evidently, it is not the tattooed ladies themselves that are especially noteworthy for they have long existed; it is the social reaction to them in former times that is remarkable.

The European astonishment at the idea of a woman being tattooed was by no means universal. Indeed, among the oldest known examples of tattooing is an Egyptian princess of the first Theban dynasty, which flourished more than 2,000 years before the birth of Christ. Her mummified remains were discovered in 1923 in a remarkably preserved condition in a tomb near Luxor, and bore several dainty tattoo marks upon one shoulder, the neck and breasts. Another and possibly even older mummified Egyptian corpse, was that of a high caste woman with patterns of dots and dashes tattooed on her lower abdomen, thighs and arms. However, despite these Theban ladies antiquity, they were not the first contact that European society had with a tattooed female - that distinction goes to an abducted Eskimo woman.

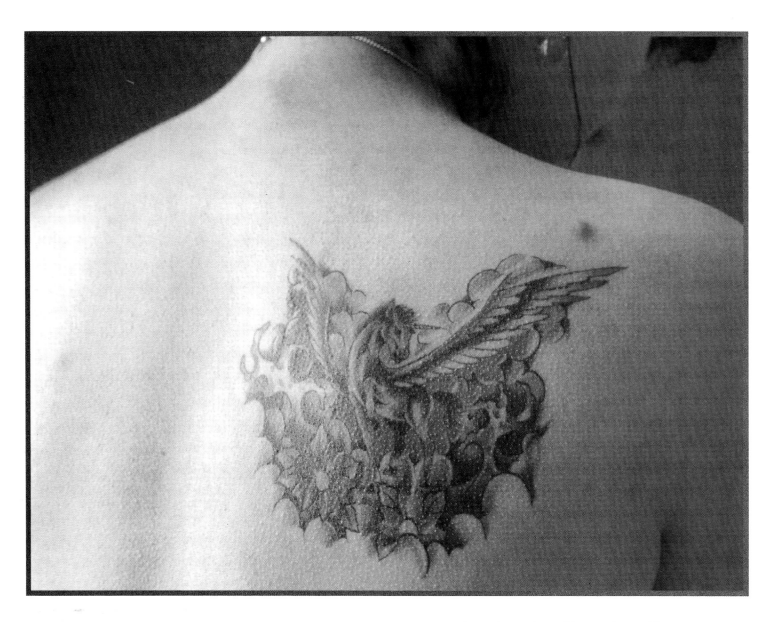

In 1578, Artic explorer Sir Martin Frobisher came upon an Eskimo woman whilst he was attempting to discover the North West Passage. The woman's face bore an elegant pattern of delicate blue-black dots aligned upon the cheeks, chin and across the forehead. Frobisher returned with her to Britain, and she is known to have been publicly exhibited in London as a curiosity, both because of her remote origins and her facial markings.

The real origins of tattooing women will probably never be known. It is not always possible to determine just how old or how widespread a social custom is, for in many societies there were no permanent records and oral history has proven inadequate to determine when a particular practice began. In other societies, practices such as tattooing apparently came and went periodically. However, it is known that women have long borne tattoos among the Ainu people of Japan, the Polynesian Islanders of the Pacific and

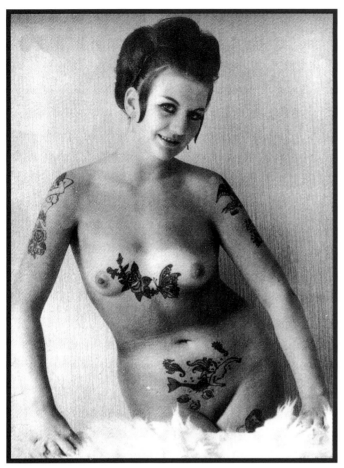

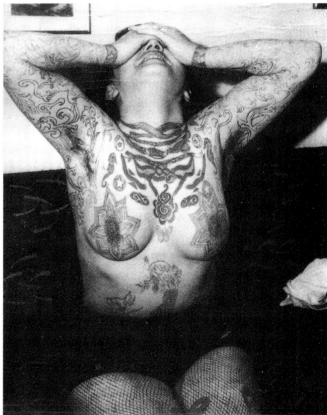

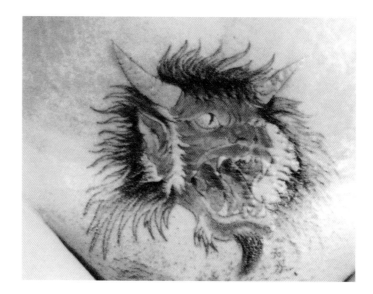

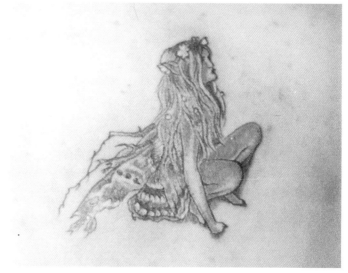

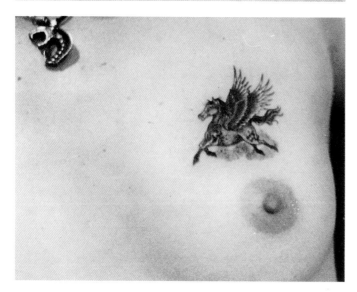

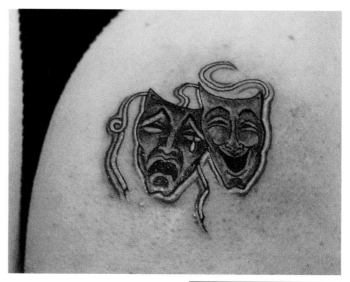

Some of the varied tattoo
designs women are
choosing these days. All by
Tony Cohen.

(Top) Bev Robinson. (Above) A postcard from the 1920s. (Top right) Bev Robinson as Cindy Ray. (Below right) Tattoos – nineteen-sixties style.

(Top) Tattoo as a decorative fashion accessory!

certain tribes of New Guinea. In each of these cases, it is reasonable to suppose that the customary tattoos date back a very long time.

The reasons behind women becoming tattooed are varied. Many of the Ainu were coastal dwelling people, and while the men were away in boats fishing, the women harvested shellfish. These women were remarkable swimmers, who traditionally swam nude and dived for shellfish - and the tattoos were regarded as a convenient and waterproof talisman which offered protection from the perils of the sea. The inland Ainu women were also tattooed, but their markings celebrated menarche, betrothal and marriage as well as being markings of tribal membership. Among New Guinean tribeswomen tattoos were a status symbol - the more tattoos a girl had, the more suitors she could expect, and the higher the bride price her father could command. Under such a social system, it is not surprising that some girls were tattooed extensively, even on the least obvious and sensitive areas of the body such as the inner thighs.

As interesting as these various customs are, it was not those women who were customarily tattooed and lived in communities where tattooing was accepted who excited

Full back Japanese tattoo of great beauty on a great beauty.

undue interest - it was the tattooing of European women which provoked the most extreme reactions, and those reactions occurred in both continental Europe and North America. The excitement these women aroused was fairly temporary - as most novelties are - but was interesting because of some the inhibited social attitudes and contrary aspects of humankind it revealed.

It is surely no coincidence that the era of interest in tattooed women occurred concurrently with the invention and patenting of the electric tattooing needle. Since the spread of any new technology was far slower in the 1890s that it is today, it is obvious that anyone who introduced a new novelty dependent upon a new invention could reap considerable commercial reward - particularly if they could introduce it in areas where the new invention was unknown. This is undoubtedly what occurred - a combination of profiteering and personal exhibitionism led to the appearance in the fairgrounds and circuses of firstly, tattooed men and shortly thereafter, of tattooed women. There can be little doubt, given the inferior social position of women at the time, that there were also some instances of coercion and exploitation in the display of tattooed ladies.

Probably the first completely tattooed lady to appear in Europe was Irene Woodward, who adopted the stage name of 'La Belle Irene' and began her public appearances in the early 1890s. She attracted enormous attention, and like other tattooed ladies of the period, was closely 'studied' by 'scientists'. Her tattoos were in a multiple design of flowers,

A tattoo of your favourite pop group, such as Motley Crue might seem a good idea now, but what happens when they slip off the record charts?

snakes, butterflies - and she claimed to have been tattooed in the remote western regions of America in an attempt to escape the sexual advances of savage Red Indians. The story was pure fabrication - a simple embroidery of her public 'act' - which was given lie by the inclusion among her tattoos of designs of angels and sanctimonious texts such as 'Never Despair' and 'Nothing Without Labour'. Clearly, these were not of Red Indian origin, but the same popular tale was nevertheless adopted by several other women with decorated bodies.

'La Belle Irene' set a trend: other tattooed ladies also tended to embroider their acts in some way. Anetta Nerona was a German lady who carried tattooed portraits of Goethe, Bismark, Schiller, Richard Wagner and Emperor Wilhelm II upon her body - but she also performed as a musician, snake charmer and magician. American Mrs Own Jensen, using the stage name 'Dainty Dotty', had her enormous 268 kilogram body extensively tattooed by her husband and appeared as the fat lady with the Ringling Bros. circus troupe. 'La Belle Angora', another tattooed lady appearing in Europe, sold printed postcards of herself as she mixed with her audience after her show. It was her habit to appear in 'lace boots' - which were actually a further example of her tattoos.

Competition was apparently fierce, for the ladies covered almost their entire bodies with tattoos - often with designs of a 'cultural' or 'patriotic' theme. Antonia Gibbons who appeared with Ringling Bros. Barnum and Bailey travelling carnival shows, had a portrait of George Washington emblazoned between her breasts, the child Jesus on her left thigh, the Madonna on her right thigh, Vermeer's Diana and the Nymphs on her right calf, Botticelli's *Annunciation* on her left arm, Michaelangelo's *Holy Family* on her biceps and Raphael's *Angels* below her left shoulder...as well as various lesser designs. elsewhere. Englishwoman Mrs Ben Corday wore a portrait of Queen Victoria on her chest surmounted by various coats of arms. Her right breast declared 'Peace' and her left breast 'Unity'. Such were the 'respectable' icons of the times.

'Respectability' was a vexing issue for these women. The tales of being tattooed by savages to distract them from rape was patently untrue, and equally obviously was an attempt to 'excuse' their tattoos - for being tattooed was an obvious and radical departure from normal in a society which rigorously espoused conformity. Society at the turn of the century was also very inhibited, indeed puritanical, about women displaying themselves - and these ladies were obliged to appear in garments which displayed their tattoos yet would normally be regarded as being scandalously licentious. The tattooed ladies were clearly uncomfortable about this matter, for illustrations of them show that the tattooing ended abruptly at the neck and wrists, thus enabling them to remain totally inconspicuous in the normal and enveloping garb of the time.

**The contrasting styles of
Japanese-influenced designs
(top) and Western (below).**

The same issue of 'respectability' helps to explain why the exhibition of tattooed ladies outlived the same type of display by menfolk - there were elements of shock and sexuality in women appearing in a semi-clothed state, irrespective of their reason for doing so. Doubtless, a male spectator at a tattooed lady show at the turn of the century would consider that he received good value for money, for he experienced the encapsulated pleasures of a striptease act, an art gallery and a burlesque show all at once! For the ladies themselves, the picture was more ambiguous: they travelled extensively, lived well, and were financially rewarded, but in choosing such a life they sacrificed social acceptability. In short, although sections of society was prepared to fete them fleetingly, overall it condemned them permanently as nonconformists. Quite quickly, tattooed ladies all but faded from the carnival scene and public consciousness, becoming just another dated novelty overwhelmed by the mass of more pressing issues of everyday life. Bev Robinson was the last lady in Australia to enlist herself in travelling side shows and has been a tattooist for many years.

In the very early years of the present century, the tattooed woman re-emerged in a different guise: as a celebrity rather than as a freak or curiosity. Prominent public figures such as politicians and business tycoons paid exorbitant sums to follow a fashion fad for intricate and unusual tattoos - and these celebrities included several women. Lady Randolph Churchill was one; she sported a tattooed armlet of a serpent eating its own tail as a symbol of eternity, a symbol which whilst it appealed to the intellect, also carried a certain sexual connotation. This was the norm: outwardly innocuous symbols with sexual connotations became popular among the female portion of the wealthy and fashionable set. Cosmetic tattooing also came into vogue. Many society belles had eyebrows darkened or cheeks reddened by means of the tattooists' needles. Like most fads, these fashions soon faded. Over-priced commercialisation of tattooing - and too often, poor execution - quickly led to a waning of its popularity and perceived desirability. By the 1920s, most of the people who had followed the brief fad were adopting a style of attire and jewellery which was designed to conceal their past decorative indiscretions.

The popularity of tattooing among women waned for several decades, but was never totally extinguished. Throughout the world during the years 1920-70, girls continued to seek tattoos which reflected their tastes and interests. Every imaginable image from hearts and flowers or from dragons and tigers through portraits of movie stars or sumo wrestlers were inked into female flesh - but the tattooed girls of these years, at least within European society, were a very small minority. Strangely, this was a period in which the popularity of tattoos was steadily increasing among men - but for women, tattooing remained a 'fringe' and 'underground' activity.

The strident cries of women for recognition of their individuality really began in the postwar period when working women gained financial independence, and these cries were subsequently unified and manifested in the global feminist movement - and the expression of the newly-recognised individuality in the form of tattooing soon followed.

Perhaps the first readily identifiable group to adopt tattoos were those strong-willed and individualistic women associated with the freedom-oriented motorcycling fraternity. Among such women, tattooing bestowed a sense of group membership as well as a sense of equality with menfolk, and so it was a practice which was swiftly adopted. Tattooing among these ladies were as varied and often as feminine, as the people who wore them.

Other women emulated them: some young, single and independent; some free-thinking housewives; yet others business tycoons with strong and influential careers. Tattooing among women was no longer a phenomenon restricted either to the depths or the pinnacle of society as it has formerly been, nor as an 'underground' interest - it had become an interest which permeated all levels of life. Women, forced by biological necessity to be always more conscious of than men that they were responsible for their own bodies, had found an acceptable way of letting their bodies reveal their individuality and spirit. Thus, all truly 'liberated' women were poised to share equally with men in the highly individual tattoo renaissance which was to quickly follow.

(Below) Ainu women with distinctive facial tattoos. Taiwan 1972.

LYDIA, THE TATTOOED LADY
By E.Y. Harburg and Harold Arlen

A famous song from the 1939 Marx Brothers film "Marx Bros. At the Circus", Lydia, The Tattooed Lady has been parodied time and again. But why? The original is funny enough.

Lydia, oh! Lydia, say you have met Lydia,
Oh! Lydia, the Tatooed lady?
She has eyes that folks adore so
And a torso even more so.
Lydia, oh! Lydia that "Encyclopedia",
Oh! Lydia, the Queen of tattoo.
On her back is the Battle of Waterloo,
Beside it the Wreck of the Hesperus, too.
And proudly above the waves the Red, White and Blue,
You can learn a lot from Lydia (*whistle*)
She can give you a view of the world in tattoo
If you step up and tell her where,
For a dime you can see Kankakee or Paree,
Or Washington crossing the Delaware (*whistle*).
Oh! Lydia, oh! Lydia, say have you met Lydia,
Oh! Lydia, the Tattooed Lady?
When her muscles start relaxin'
Up the hill comes Andrew Jackson,
Lydia, oh! Lydia, that "encyclopedia",
Oh! Lydia, the champ, of them all.
For two bits she will do a Mazurka in Jazz,
With a view of Niag'ra that no artist has,
And on a clear day you can see Alcatraz,
You can learn a lot from Lydia.
La-la-la, La-la-la, La-la-la, La-la-la,
Come along and see Buff'lo Bill with his lassoo,
Just a little classic by Mendel Picasso;
Here is Captain Spaulding exploring the Amazon,
And Godiva, but with her pajamas on.
La-la-la, La-la-la, La-la-la, La-la-la,
Here is Governor Whalen unveilin' the Trylon,
Over on the west coast we have Treasure Islan'.
Here's Nijinsky a-doin' the Rhumba,
Here's her Social Security numba.
La-la-la, La-la-la, La-la-la, La-la-la,
Lydia, oh! Lydia, say you have met Lydia,
Oh! Lydia, the champ of them all.
She once swept an Admiral clear off his feet,
The ships on her hips made his heart skip a beat,
And now the old boy's in command of the fleet,
For he went and married Lydia.

INTERNATIONAL TATTOO GALLERY

Tattoo art is international. The pictures in this section are typical of the work that is being performed around the world. Most of it beautiful and much of it astonishing. Modern practitioners are innovative in terms of design, colour and style. Today no subject is taboo, and tattooists and clients are responding to the challenge. Whether you yearn for a tattoo of a monster or a hand grenade, somewhere, someone is waiting to do it for you.

American Ed Hardy was responsible for the tattooing of this spectacular creature for Bill Salmon, of San Francisco.

(Top) Tony Cohen with Ed Hardy at the 1994 San Francisco Tattoo Convention, and (below) with Jack Rudy.

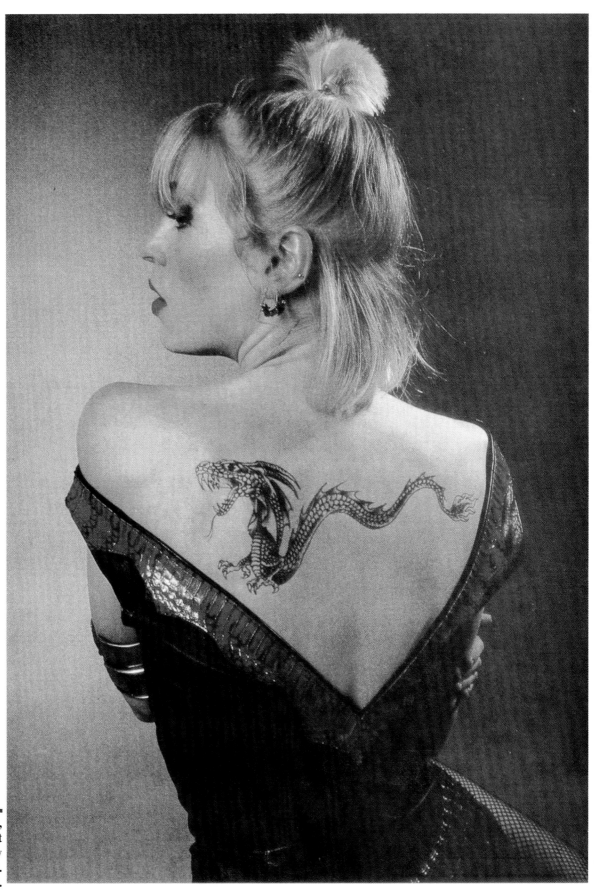

A simple,
truly elegant
design by
Hanky Panky.
1982.

Photograph opposite :
by Keith Cole

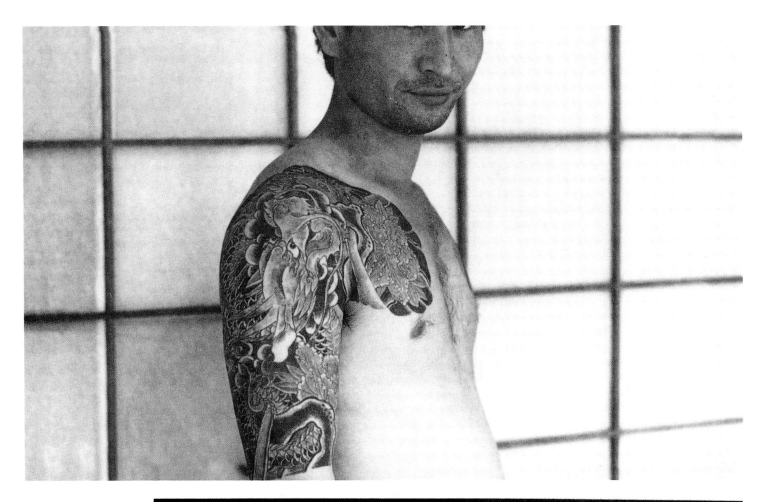

Two examples of Cliff Raven's work - the designs are bold and striking but with perhaps less use of strong colours than normal.

Tattoo by Dennis Cockell,
Great Britain.

FELIX, LORETTA, & FILIP LEU

ARTISTES DE TATOUAGE

34, RUE CENTRALE (3e étage)
La maison à côté du bar «CASH CLUB»
LAUSANNE 1003
– SWITZERLAND –

Ouvert: à partir de 15 h. jusqu'à 23 h.
Tous les vendredis - samedis - dimanches et lundis
Fermé: les mardis, mercredis et jeudis

TATTOOING'S NEW WAVE

For many years tattooists tended to use a limited range of designs, but of late a number of innovative tattooists have revolutionised the art, extending the boundaries of design, colour and form. Influenced by Japanese and Celtic motifs these artists have created tattooing's new wave.

Throughout the world, attitudes towards tattooing have varied as greatly as the form and subject matter of the tattoos themselves. Yet tattoos, whether seen simply as oddities, decoration or a unique form of serious art, has survived.

Some societies have praised and admired the skills and styles of indigenous tattoo art; other societies have succeeded in deliberately eradicating all traces of ancient tattoo rituals, perhaps seeing in them some obscure threat to their changed social structures. In yet other societies, tattooing survived, but only as an oddity rather than as the readily recognisable cultural feature that it had formerly been.

Most of the styles of the past were simply decorative patterns, while others developed into stylised pictorial art, but both were often confined to relatively small areas of the body. Only among the Polynesian peoples of the Pacific region was there an early tattooing culture which significantly altered a person's entire appearance. Tattoo art has long been seen a limited diversity but an almost unlimited adversity.

Many argument have been advanced against tattooing, most of them fallacious. The 'religious' argument that tattooing is a desecration of the body - seen either as God's

Design by Fran.

**Print by Doc Price,
Plymouth. U.K.**

earthly temple or more simply as a direct gift from God - is clearly wrong. Some pious people, such as Coptic Christians, adopt tattooed crucifixes as an expression of the depth of their faith. Further, if interference with the body is sacrilegious, how can surgery (particularly amputations or plastic surgery), curative skin pharmacy or the manufacture of either cosmetics or prostheses be defended?

Another argument advanced is that tattooing is unhygienic - indeed, in 1961 the City of New York sharply restricted tattooing on the grounds that tattooing needles were instrumental in the spread of hepatitis. Today, the same fear is voiced concerning the spread of AIDS. The truth is that tattooists can and do sanitise and disinfect their instruments as readily, and as often as, for example, dentists, beauticians, podiatrists or even hairdressers.

A further argument concerns the permanence of tattooing - many people feel that to alter themselves in an irreversible way may bring regrets later in life. Again one can point to unchallenged additions; stomach tucks, and implants are just as dangerous, and in some cases, far more dangerous. Nor is the matter of making an irreversible choice confined to bodily concerns - an unwise choice in matters of career, cash management or matrimony can bring far greater regrets later in life than a simple matter of tattooing.

Yet despite the inherent weaknesses of the arguments against it, in most societies tattooing remains a generally frowned upon fringe activity. Because of this, it has been isolated from the mainstream of more conventional art - but it now steadily gaining more recognition as a unique, difficult, disciplined and legitimate art form. Indeed, a new

Print by Ed Hardy.
U.S.A.

wave of interest in tattooing has mounted, and is currently sweeping across much of the planet.

There are now magazines devoted to tattooing, museums of past tattoo patterns and implements, organised and competitive exhibitions of the tattooists' skills and many more serious books devoted to the subject. With the increase in the general awareness of what tattoo art is about has come an increase in the number of people choosing to become artistically tattooed subjects. No longer do tattooists see mainly callow youths seeking some stereotyped expression of their emergent masculinity - more frequently they are seeing more mature adults from many social strata who are seeking designs which express varied facets of their individuality and humanity. More people of both genders are now making the transition, as aware individuals, from naive Naked Ape to the more sophisticated Illustrated Man. Their intent is to prove that human art can refine, improve and enhance the appearance of the human body.

The resurgence of interest in tattoo art is not merely a reflection of people possessing more disposable income, or of developed marketing skills, nor even just greater demand for decoration than an increased general level of sophistication brings. It is above all else, a reflection of great developments that have occurred within the art of tattooing itself.

Formerly, those who sought tattoos did so on a piecemeal basis; a small and complete picture was tattooed on some part of the body and at a later date, another small and complete design was tattooed elsewhere. Inevitably, where tattooing continued over a prolonged period, the final result was usually a collage of discrete and unassociated elements - often lacking in aesthetic value. Tattoo studios catered to those trends; they possessed large catalogues of small and complete designs and so rarely worked on a large scale, or a unified basis.

Of course, some people choose to have a small and simple design and these were available. Increasingly, however, even small designs are no longer stereotypes dictated by the catalogues; clients demand an original design which will remain both personal and unique. Indeed, some people become collectors; their bodies show a variety of subjects in a variety of styles applied by several renowned tattoo artists.

Also increasingly, clients are seeking larger designs to cover specific portions of their anatomy, and the tattooist's vocabulary, reflects this: 'full back', 'quarter body' and

Print by Kazuo Oguri.
Gifu City. Japan.

Tattoo by Filip Leu.
Lausanne,
Switzerland.

By Tony Cohen.

Kazuo Oguri's design is a very funny example of Japanese erotic tattoo art.

'sleeve' are becoming common descriptive terms. Such large tattoos are often complex designs presenting many intricate elements in a pleasingly unified manner - and many are intended to be integrated into larger, more complicated compositions. These demand more of the tattoo artist than just the intellectual and aesthetic skill; empathy with the client's desires - both immediate and overall - and technical excellence are both vital prerequisistes to an artisitic and mutually satisfying result.

Clearly, a comprehensive understanding of human anatomy, and well developed skills are of paramount importance; tattooists cannot erase an inadvertent error, must work slowly to allow healing, and are challenged by the multi-curved and pliant nature of the surface worked upon. They must also consider the dynamic nature of their surface, for a design should remain pleasing from all angles of view and despite natural human movements. Tattooing well demands a high degree of discipline from the practitioner as well as the client.

Because these large tattoos are truly original and highly personal decorations, they are frequently laden with a symbolism determined by the wearer; a reflection of some

Flowers have always been a popular subject for tattoos. Nowadays there is a trend towards realistic renderings rather than the stylised roses of the past. This unfinished Waratah is a fine example of modern flower rendering.

aspect of that personality or psyche. They are the result of a close relationship between the subject, symbolism, wearer and tattooist's interpretation. As such and given the need for discipline and the high degree of skill involved in their creation, there can be little valid argument that the results achieved truly merit the appellation of 'art'.

This new wave of 'new' art is international in nature, with artists in several countries continually redefining the boundaries of tattoo art – frequently with stunning and very successful results. After so many decades of stereotyping through the use of pattern catalogues, this is a refreshing and healthy development. Again distinctive styles are emerging, not along the cultural lines of former times, but according to the whim of talented individuals and the wishes of clients with a more acute sense of artistic values. Such a trend should prove beneficial to all tattoo devotees, for new approaches cater to a wider range of tastes, suggest newer directions still, and so will assist in promoting a greater appreciation and acceptance of tattoo art.

Some of the more noted tattoo artists, many refining techniques or developing new styles, have established in-

ternational reputations and draw their clientele from all over the world. Among them are people such as Don Ed Hardy, Cliff Raven, Jack Rudy, Bob Olson, Jonathon Shaw, Bill Salmon, Leo Zuluetta, Henry Golfield, Don Thome, Spider Webb, Karl Barber, Vivyn Lazonga and Shotsie Gorman (all of the United States of America); Nakano, Horiyoshi, Horikin (Mitsuaki Owada), Horishiba and Horigoro in Japan; Englishmen George Burchett, Les Skuse, Rich Mingins, Doc Price, Jerry Wrigley, Mickey Sharpz and Ian of Reading; Danes Jorgen Kinshausen and Jorgen Kristiansen; Filip Leu in Switzerland; Berni Luther and Klaus and Jorgan Fuhrmann in Germany. Some of the outstanding tattoo artists in Australia to win public recognition and acclaim from the tattooing fraternity are Les Bowen, Danny Robinson, Dutchy Cornellison, Patsy Farrow and Colin Creed. Numerous others are achieving similar high standards, and although most tattooists derive much of their custom through word of mouth recommendations rather than through extensive advertising, they may usually be contacted through the specialist magazines.

Branded!

TATTOOIST TONY FINDS WOMEN ARE BEING DRAWN TO USE HIS SERVICES

By Tony Maguire

NEXT TIME you walk down the street, consider this — above the left breast of the girl at the bus stop may be a large tattoo of a Bengal tiger.

More and more women are getting their bodies "branded" with tattoos. And the designs are increasingly intricate, covering a much larger skin area than in the past.

On the way out are the hearts inscribed "Fred" and suchlike of yesteryear. On the way in are multi-coloured works of skin art which sometimes stretch from neck to navel.

East Sydney tattooist Tony Cohen says half his customers are women and the majority of them are secretaries, nurses and other professional types.

Tigers are very much in vogue with the female tattoo set at present, reports Tony, whose parlour is called The Illustrated Man (the day may not be far off when he changes it to The Illustrated Person).

Tattooist Fran Sayer, who works for Tony, is probably Australia's most illustrated woman. Dragon faces, crouching cheetahs, galloping horses and cascading waterfalls — and more — adorn her body.

Fran and Tony consider themselves artists; their medium just happens to be skin and ink. They get a lot of creative satisfaction out of what they do and earn more from it than the average artist working on canvas and other non-living materials.

Says Tony: "It's the rough stuff which turns people off tattoos. I'm always doing cover-up jobs for people who've done them themselves or gone to an amateur.

◄ Like diamonds, tattoos are forever. So Tony can't afford to make a boob, even though this customer's tatts (left) may not be widely seen.

Australia's most decorated lady, Fran Sayer (right) works for Tony. They see themselves as artists — and they find their creativity pays. ►

Media Fascination

We are all used to the phenonomen of media-hype. The relentless pursuit of a story that blows it out of all proportion to its intrinsic worth. While the media's attitude to tattooing probably isn't in that class, over the years it has come in for more than its fair share of media attention. Partly, of course, the reason reflects society's interest in the unusual, risque and forbidden, and partly because tattooing is such a graphic, visual thing that it works well in colour magazines and on television. If the writer and photographer can find a grotesque angle, so much the better. With the rise of the alternative life-style and music magazines tattooing has been written about less to shock than inform and the publication of specialist tattooing magazines has provided a forum for comment and discussion as unbalanced in its way as that in the main-stream press. That may be because tattooing tends to polarise opinion, for and against.

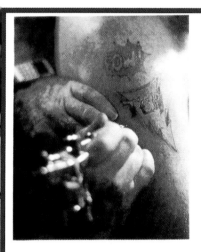

TATTOO YOU

Love 'em or loathe 'em, tattoos will leave you marked for life. Clinton Walker knows — he has two...

IT takes a lot of time to get up the nerve, like talking to a girl for the first time. This can't be a passing fancy. If you want to tattoo, you better realise it's for keeps.

So you might cruise past what used to be called a tattoo parlour and is now a studio, trying to summon up the courage to go inside. You check out the clientele, a motley assortment of skin-heads and bikies, and think, I'm not like these guys...

Finally you decide you won't be satisfied until you get it done, so you cross the threshold, put your money down and *do it.*

And you've just broken a very real taboo. Tattoos are for bikies and skinheads, boxers and truck drivers. *Nice* boys do not have tattoos, even if they're currently kinda fashionable. I mean, Johnny

There's always the classic tattoo designs , the skulls and crossbones and 'Death Before Dishonour' scrolls, but what's emerged lately is a more personalised approach to designs: Marijuana leaves and the Rolling Stones' Jaggerlips logo were popular back in the '70s. The first tattoo I had done myself, in 1981, was a Batman-style "Pow!"

Getting tattooed isn't a hard thing to do. It doesn't cost much, and it doesn't really hurt. The hard part is getting past the taboo; this life-long marking is going to send some people into paroxysms of resentment and contempt.

Make sure you think long and hard about your tattoo. Whacking your current girlfriend's name on your arm might seem like a

The Birth

Of a

Tattoo

Tattoo by Tony Cohen.

The Developing

Tattoo

Tattoo by Tony Cohen.

Thousands of young European girls are getting their bodies tattooed with all kinds of decorations. They think it looks nice but'....

by Geoff Hawk

MEN HATE TATTOOED WOMEN

The tattooing craze is once again sweeping England and Europe. It seems that every few years the novelty rebounds with increased popularity. This time however, it

snakes imprinted across their back or on the lower thigh. The men claim it detracts from femininity

"Young sailors go to a tattooist as part of a ritual that separates the men from the boys. 60 per cent

of advertising his busi..ess, told Flame that tattooing will never die out because there will always be people,

He said many peopl revealed their character i the selection of a design Those who had MOTHE

Wonderful stuff isn't it? Why let the facts get in the way of a good story? Ask enough people and you'll get the answer you want. There is no doubt that some men do hate women with tattoos, but others love them. There's enough room for everyone, so why is it that some people feel that they have to denigrate what they don't like, or understand?

Some people don't like tattoos. Others don't like cricket or football. So what? Perhaps it is about time people who do like tattoos demanded equal space in the papers.

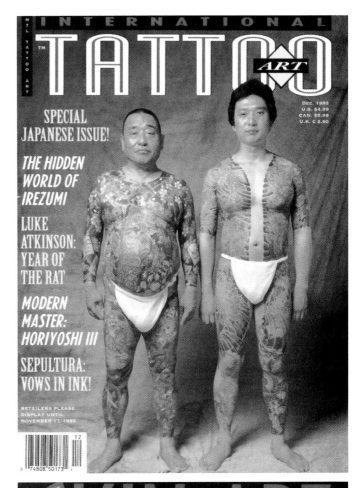

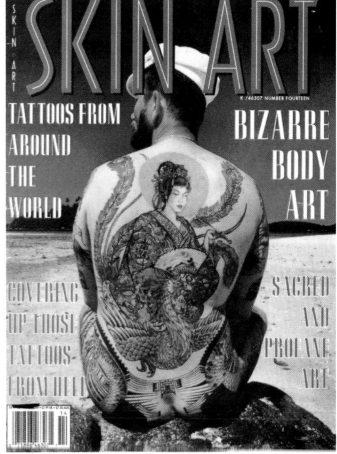

The *Tattoo Historian* (above) was a quarterly publication founded in 1982 by the Tattoo Art Museum in San Francisco, with Lyle Tuttle as editor, which attempted to address the history and culture of tattooing in an unsensational and slightly academic manner. It also attempted to give tattooing credibility by encouraging serious art institutions, such as the Massachusetts College Of Art to exhibit tattoo-related shows. The magazines (opposite and overleaf) are all high quality glossy publications dedicated to promoting tattooing. Like other specialist publications their editorial stance varies – in these cases from serious discusssions on tattooing as an art form to overt promotion of an alternative life-style. What they have in common is lots and lots of photographs of tattoos and interviews with tattooists from around the world. There's probably not a better way of keeping up to date with who is doing what to whom. *Tattoos For Men* (overleaf) has a 'sister' publication – *Tattoos For Women*, which is a little curious in this day and age. Biker life-style magazines like *Australian Easyriders* (overleaf) are also sympathetic to tattooing and often carry articles featuring tattoo spreads.

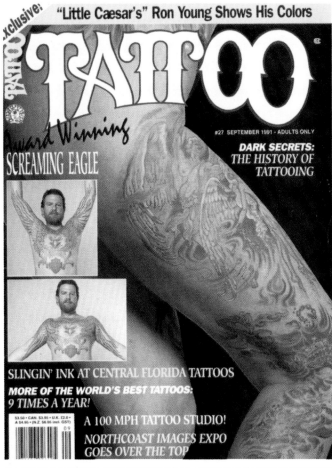

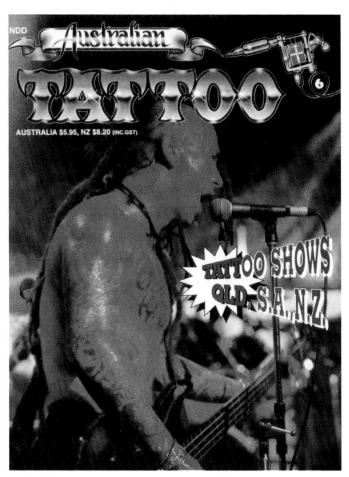

Tex takes off tats!

ON THE subject of tattoo-removing, Tex "Tall Tale" Tyrell swears he's telling the absolute truth.

"I've discovered a way to remove tattoos without leaving scarring in its place," claims Tex. "And this is no tall tale."

Colin "Tex" Tyrell, also known as "Tall Tale Tex" through his legendary reputation as a marathon yarn-spinner, has applied for a patent on a chemical solution which he believes to be the best method yet devised for the removal of unwanted tattoos.

The chemical, known at present simply as "tattoo removal solution", is planned to be distributed to authorised tattooists all around Australia.

Ironically, professional tattooists are the only people Tex will allow to use the solution for tattoo removals.

"It sounds strange, but with this chemical, tattoos can only be removed by a tattoo needle and it's best that only skilled tattooists are involved," Tex ex-

★ Tex as he was 30 years ago . . . he got rid of the face tattoos in four days.

plained from his Beenleigh (Q) home.

The story of Tex Tyrell's search for a relatively painless and non-scarring method of getting rid of tats he no longer wanted goes way back to the early 1960s when he was about to embark on a showbusiness career as "The World's Most Tattooed Man".

He was in Auckland, New Zealand, and had just had a

By ALAN VEITCH
Photos by:
RICHARD CAMPION

series of tattoos put on his face — a butterfly tattoo across his nose, two fighting eagles on his forehead, robin redbreasts on either side of his nose and a pair of cobra snakes on his cheeks. He was quite a sight.

Then the showbiz deal fell through!

"I heard about a plastic surgeon in Auckland who was supposed to be one of the best in the world for doing a removal job, but when I went to see him he told me the waiting list was six months long.

"I waited the six months and when I went to see the plastic surgeon again he told me I might have to wait another six months because his main priority was working on accident cases, whereas my problem with the tattoos was my own fault.

"Well, I decided to take the matter into my own hands. I'd have to work out a way to get the face-tattoos off all by myself."

So Tex read books on tattoo removal and came upon a particular chemical.

The chemical solution could only be administered through a tattoo needle — so Tex acquired a bottle of the solution, tested it . . . and off came the face tattoos!

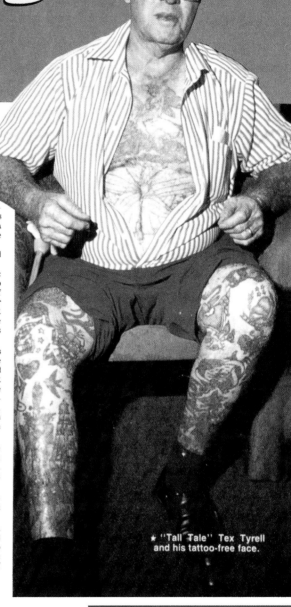

★ "Tall Tale" Tex Tyrell and his tattoo-free face.

Perhaps the last word in this brief look at the media's love affair with tattooing should be given to removing tattoos. This is an ongoing subject beloved of journalists and sub-editors who can't resist headlines like "Ta-ta, Tats", "Scarred For Life", "The Sad Badge of Shame", but "Tall Tale Tex's" tale from the *Australasian Post* of July 4, 1982 is a masterpiece of alliteration and of the old adage of sensation the norm, accuracy the exception!

INSTRUMENTS of DeliqHT

The earliest tattooing instruments probably didn't differ very much from some of the instruments still used by primitive peoples today. Sharpened animal or fish bones, sharpened bamboo slivers, fragments of shell, thorns, tapped into the flesh with a stone or other weight. Specialised tools were developed by the Maoris for their *Moko* tattooing, which involves gouging into the flesh and by the Japanese who used clusters of up to forty needles, but in the main the principle of pricking the skin by hand remained much the same for thousands of years until the invention of the electric tattooing machine late last century. Since then it has been modified, re-designed, and tinkered with but in the end it does the same job as the fish bone - makes little hole in the skin for the pigment, whether it's a modern non-toxic colour or burnt ash.

S F REILLY'S TATTOOING MACHINE.

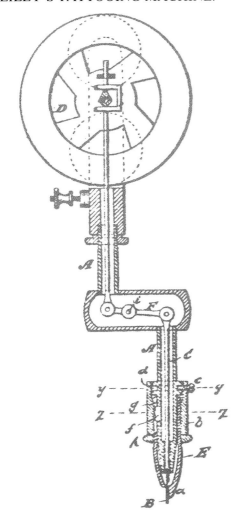

The modern electric tattooing machine owes its origins to inventor Thomas Edison's Autographic Printer of 1875 and the Electric Stencil Pen which he patented in 1877. Both of these devices were designed for hard surface engraving such as metals. It was later adapted for tattooing - the first mention in print of this appears to have been in 1884. The man mentioned in this article was S.F. Reilly, who was issued a patent for a tattooing machine on 8 December 1891.

The patent covered only the tube as the power source was identical to Edison's Autographic Printer. Reilly's modifications increased the stroke of the machine making it more suited for use on skin and making it faster to use. While an example of the Edison Stencil Pen has survived it is not known whether any of Reilly's devices are still around.

Since then the machines have been steadily improved so that today's machines are virtually painless and fast. The needles puncture the skin 1,000 to 3,000 times a minute, penetrating less than a quarter of a millimetre - just deep enough to ensure permanence of the design.

Commercial machines have been available since Reilly started manufacture, but many tattoo artists have, and still do, build their own, confident that their improvements are better than the mass produced items.

All of them operate on the same principle, with the needles being driven forward and retracted by the action of a spring (or in some cases, a rubber band), activated by the switching on an off of a pair of magnets.

Most western tattooists use two machines - one with two to four needles for outlining and a second with from six to twelve needles for shading.

In other parts of the world, either by choice or because of

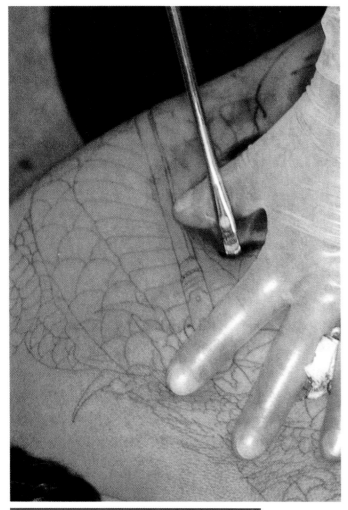

the lack of electricty hand tattoo implements are still used. Many Japanese tattoo artists still prefer the traditional hand tools using needle closters which contain as many as 40 needles to achieve the delicate shading of tone and colour that are so much a feature of Japanese tattooing.

Along with other users of hand tattoo tools, the Japanese masters also use single needles, especially for outlining the design. Great skill is needed to use hand tools effectively and in shading large areas, the right wrist action is important.

The electric tattoo machine was developed in order to simplify and speed up the process, so even in Japan the trend is towards their use. Most machines are intended to be used with a 24 or 12 volt transformer but battery powered models have been developed - the first Edison gadgets were battery powered - for use away from the mains.

One of the best known manufacturers of tattooing machines was The Zeis Studio of Rockford, Illinois. During the Second World War they redesigned a machine made by a legend in the business names Bill Jones. In 1941 they made enough parts for 1500 machines - selling the last one in 1966. Curiously the first two machines they delivered were returned. It's no wonder that Zeis thought that they would be stuck with the whole 1500.

(Top) Traditional Western Samoan tattoo instruments. (Above) Japanese hand tattoo needle in use and (right) the logo of the American Zeis company – not to be confused with the German optical firm, Zeiss.

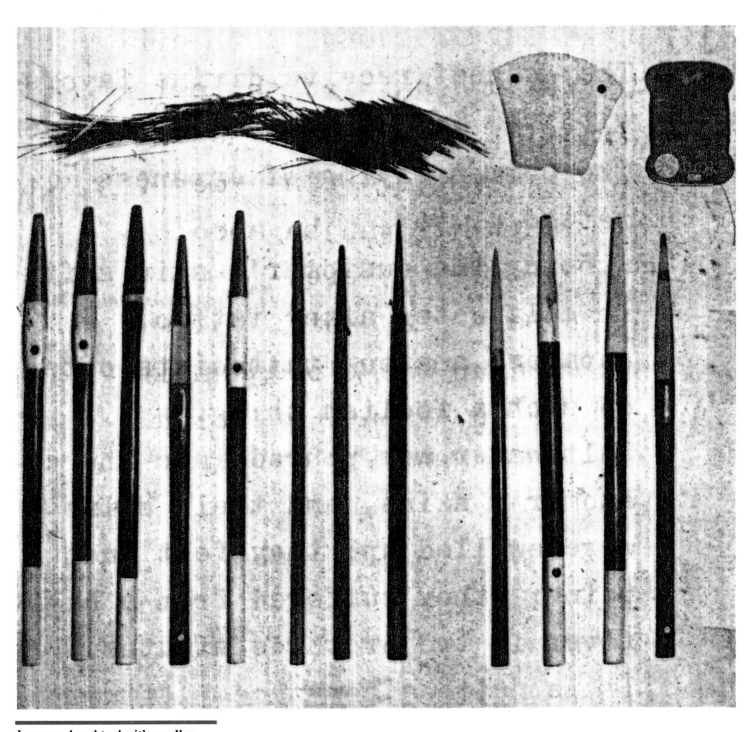

Japanese hand tool with needles and thread. Artists who still use these hand tools use five needles for outlining and five needles for shading. The needles are fastened to bamboo or ivory handles with thread. The tattooist varies the thickness of the line using the same needles, but for delicate black shading switches to a set-up with 15 needles in an upper row and 15 in a lower, which is very fast in the hands of a skilled tattooist.

WATERS SPECIAL NO. 4
1928 Model

The first and principal requirement of a tattooing instrument is durability. You will note from this illustration (MY NEW IDEAS) instead of the usual connecting posts being on the back, they are fitted close on the side, which balances the instrument, featuring the particular improvement along with the long stroke adjustment and direct or short connections soldered, instrument has more kick on less power. Frame is solid casting made of Malleable Iron annealed, impossible to break. The Magnets are stamped

WATERS MF'G, DETROIT

This certifies where they were made. All parts properly fitted. Instrument is adjusted, ready for use. Connecting cord included.

Price, outliner or shader, $5.00 each.

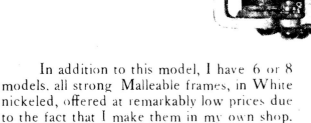

"WATERS MADE" TATTOOING Machines have been favorably known to the Tattooing trade for many years because they stand the severe strain to which they are subjected.

In addition to this model, I have 6 or 8 models, all strong Malleable frames, in White nickeled, offered at remarkably low prices due to the fact that I make them in my own shop.

I repair all makes of Tattooing machines, with a reasonable charge for my labor.

The SZ #6 STORY

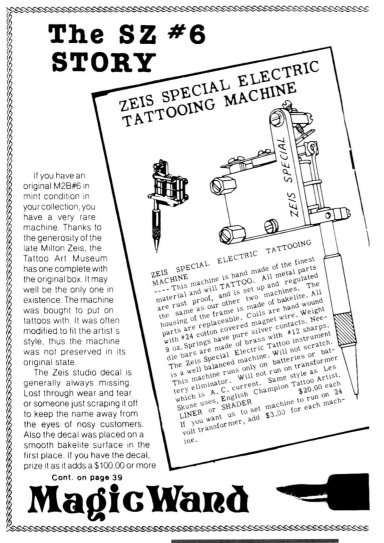

ZEIS SPECIAL ELECTRIC TATTOOING MACHINE

If you have an original M2B#6 in mint condition in your collection, you have a very rare machine. Thanks to the generosity of the late Milton Zeis, the Tattoo Art Museum has one complete with the original box. It may well be the only one in existence. The machine was bought to put on tattoos with. It was often modified to fit the artist's style, thus the machine was not preserved in its original state.

The Zeis studio decal is generally always missing. Lost through wear and tear, or someone just scraping it off to keep the name away from the eyes of nosy customers. Also the decal was placed on a smooth bakelite surface in the first place. If you have the decal, prize it as it adds a $100.00 or more

ZEIS SPECIAL ELECTRIC TATTOOING MACHINE ---- This machine is hand made of the finest material and will TATTOO. All metal parts are rust proof, and is set up and regulated the same as our other two machines. The housing of the frame is made of bakelite. All parts are replaceable. Coils are hand wound with #24 cotton covered magnet wire. Weight 9 oz. Springs have pure silver contacts. Needle bars are made of brass with #12 sharps. The Zeis Special Electric Tattoo instrument is a well balanced machine. Will not scratch. This machine runs only on batteries or battery eliminator. Will not run on transformer which is A. C. current. Same style as Les Skuse uses, English Champion Tattoo Artist. LINER or SHADER $20.00 each If you want us to set machine to run on 24 volt transformer, add $3.00 for each machine.

Cont. on page 39

MagicWand

(Below) The Spaulding Supreme Outliner with a stainless steel open sanitary tube. Cost was $37.00 in 1970.

Dear Tattoo Artist:

Articles not listed in Catalog No. 15

Contact Tips for springs	.60 doz.
Paynes Grey Water Color	1.00 tube
French Crayon Sauce	1.00 stick
Chrome-plated Needle Bars	.50 each
Machine Frames, not drilled	1.00 each
Machine Frames, Drilled & Tapped	2.50 each
Machine Frames, D & T, Chr.-pltd.	4.00 each
Chrome-plated Armature Bars	1.25 each
24-V AC Transformers	7.50
Vibro Tool—Stencil Cutter	9.95
Engraver Tube & Bar for standard Tattoo Machine for cutting stencils	5.00
5000 Hand painted designs	.15 each
Chrome-plated Needle Bars, plain	.50 each
Pure Silver Contact Screws, 1 in. x 6/36	.50
500 Used Design Sheets	.50 & up
4000 Used Stencils	.15 each
Used Tattoo Machines	10.00 & up
Used Tubes, Liners, Shaders	.75
Switchboard with rheostat	15.00
Special Small Oven-size 12"-7"-5" for sterilizing needle bars, Machine with tube and all colors	25.00
3-D Camera f3.5 Lenses	49.00
P.D.Q. Camera f4.5 Lenses	95.00
Exakta Camera 35mm f2.8 lens with case and Flash Gun	175.00

**The ZEIS Studio
728 Lesley Avenue
Rockford, Illinois**

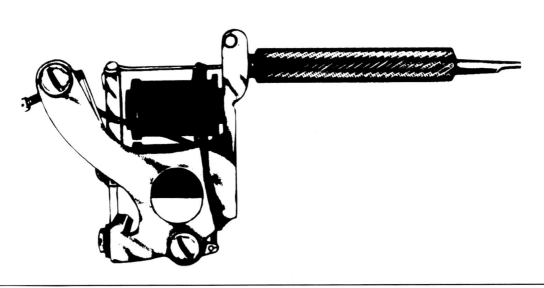

There is a wide range of gear available in Australia including locally made equipment, as these two ads from the Professional Tattooing Association of Australia magazine shows.

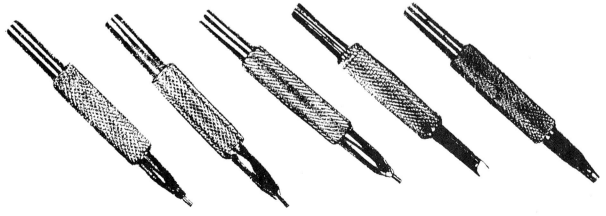

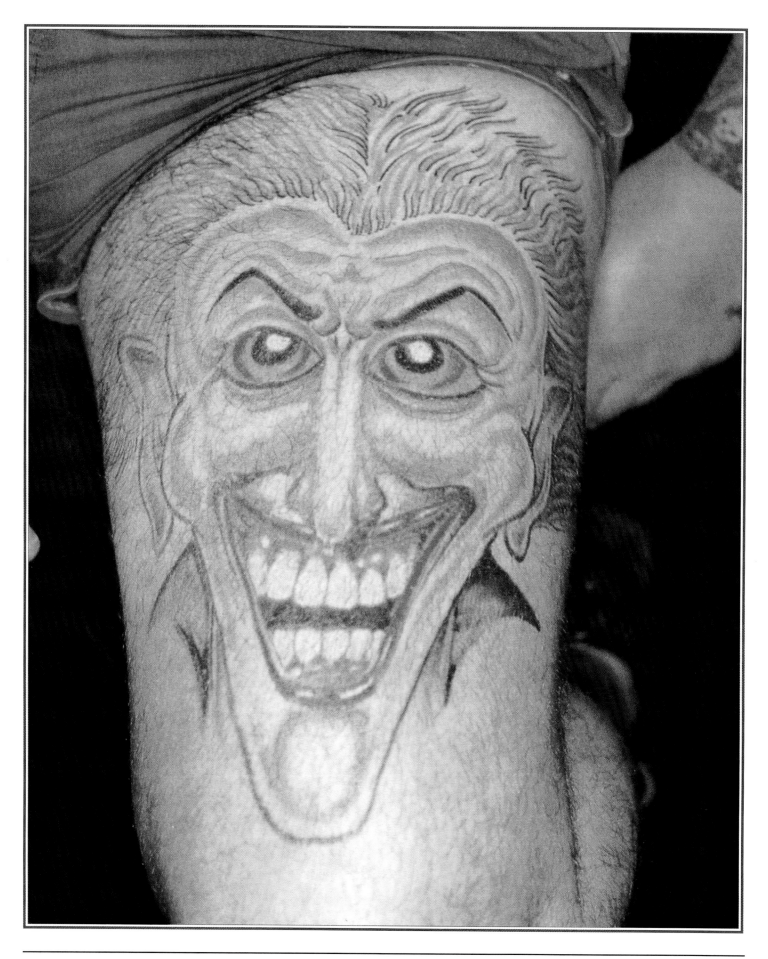

Stars Upon Thar's

Elvis, Marilyn, Laurel and Hardy, Bob Marley, Jimi Hendrix, Motely Crue, Alice Cooper, Francis Farmer, John Wayne, Charles Bronson, Brigitte Bardot, Jack Nicholson, Vincent Price, Freddie Mercury, Caesar Romeo, David Bowie, Fred Gywnne, Roy Orbison, Robert Englund, Dr Who, Jane Fonda, Anthony Hopkins, Salvador Dali, Bryan Ferry, Marlene Dietrich, Popeye, The Joker have, or all had two things in common. They were all stars or comic book characters, and they've all been the subject of tattoos. There's no doubt that other heart throbs have made it onto someone's body - it's hard to imagine that Sophia Loren, the Beatles, Meatloaf or Robert Redford have been ignored. Or Lassie and Rin Tin Tin, if it comes to that. All of us, are to some degree star-struck, but people who are into self-decoration through tattoo art are more likely to express their feelings in a tangible form. Some of the images are portraits of quite extraordinary power and have captured the essence of the subject in an uncanny manner.

(Opposite page) Tattoo by Lal Hardy, London.
(Above) Both tattoos by Nutz, Victoria.

Tattoo by Ja...
Rudy. U.S

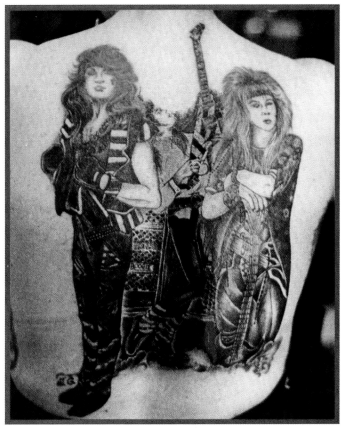

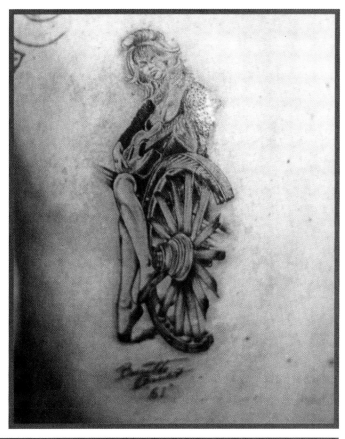

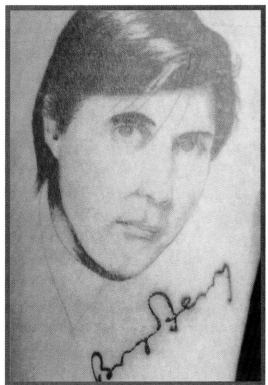

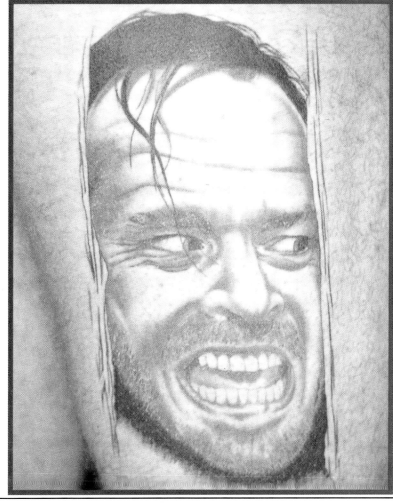

(Top right) Brigitte Bardot and (Top left) Motley Crue by Tony Cohen, Sydney. (Above) Bryan Ferry U.K., Jack Nicholson (Right) by Darren Stares, Portsmouth U.K.

Tattoo by Tin Tin,
Toulouse, France.

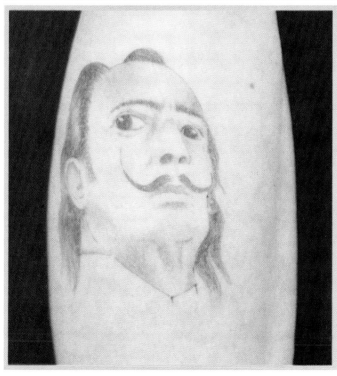

(Top) Laurel and Hardy by
Darren Stares, Portsmouth, U.K.
(Left) Miss Roxy/Salvador Dali by
Mike Malone, U.S.A
(Right) "Hannibal The Cannibal".

(Top) Motley Crue by
Tony Cohen .

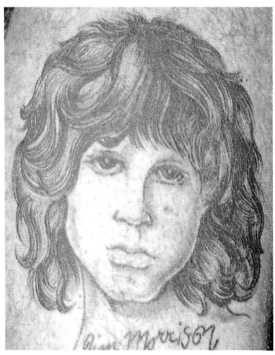

(Bottom left) Jim Morison by Les Bowen.
(Bottom right) Jimi Hendrix by Tony
Cohen. Malcolm MacDowell in
"Clockwork Orange" tattooed by
Miss Roxy (Opposite page).

Ads, Cards & Memorabilia

The explosion of interest in tattooing has led to an increased interest in collecting all kinds of related memorabilia. Most of it, apart from the tattoos themselves, tends to be of an ephemeral nature - posters, advertisements, business cards, menus, invitations, newsletters, stickers - which have the advantage of being free, or very inexpensive to acquire. Yet they serve to bring the widespread world of tattooing a little closer. So that enthusiasts in Australia, or in other countries can participate in the wider movement. For many people, like Tony Cohen, these items are keepsakes of their travels and reminders of people they have met and friends they have made. One of the great things about collecting this material is its diversity and because of its very nature the chances are that it will be creative, innovative and interesting. Just like tattoos.

TAZZ & PERCH

Members
S.A.P.T.A.
P.T.A.A.

316 NORTH EAST RD,
KLEMZIG, S.A. 5087
Ph (08) 266 3797

TATTOO ARTS '93 FESTIVAL

NOVEMBER 19th, 20th and 21st, 1993
Fri. & Sat. 10 a.m. – 12 a.m., Sun. 10 a.m. – 6 p.m.

RICHMOND, VIRGINIA
Holiday Inn Koger Center

Live Tattooing • Contests • Leather
Fun • Piercing • Jewelry • Party • Music

For more information contact:

B.I.R.D. Productions
3910 Hull Street Road, Circle Shopping Center
Richmond, Virginia 23224

Blood 'n Ink Productions • 804/528-3212
Red Dragon Tattoo Studio • 804/230-7908

TATTOO EXPO

PRIMA CONVENZIONE INTERNAZIONALE DI TATUAGGI IN ITALIA

13 e 14 novembre 1993
BOLOGNA

CONTACT: MARCO LEONI, "BODY MARKING," VIA FONDAZZA, 4S, BOLOGNA, ITALY.

PERFORMANCE DEI MIGLIORI TATUATORI INTERNAZIONALI, FRA I QUALI

HANKY PANKY di Amsterdam, **TIN TIN** di Parigi,
BERNI LUTHER di Vienna, **JONATHANSHAW** di N.Y.City
e tanti altri, Italiani e stranieri

Per informazioni: **BODY DECORATORES TATTOO STUDIO**
VIA AVESELLA 20c - Bologna, Telefono 051 - 220406 - FAX 51220406

FIERA DI BOLOGNA - SALA POLIVALENTE - P.ZZA DELLA COSTITUZIONE

233

Moon Over Miami
Tattoo Studio
14906 West Dixie Highway-
NE 149th Street
North Miami, Florida USA
33181
Hours: 12 Noon-12 Mid.
   Mon.-Sat.
   1 PM-6 PM Sun.
Phone: (305) 944-0888

Tattoos by Lou
of South Beach
231 14th Street
South Miami Beach, Florida,
USA 33139
Hours: 12 Noon-12 Mid.
   Mon.-Sat.
   1 PM-6 PM Sun.
Phone: (305) 532-7300

Tattoos by Lou
9300 South Dixie Highway, Cutler Ridge
South Miami, Florida, USA 33156
Hours: 12 Noon-8PM Mon.-Fri.
12 Noon-6PM Sat., 1PM-6PM Sun. Phone (305) 238-8333

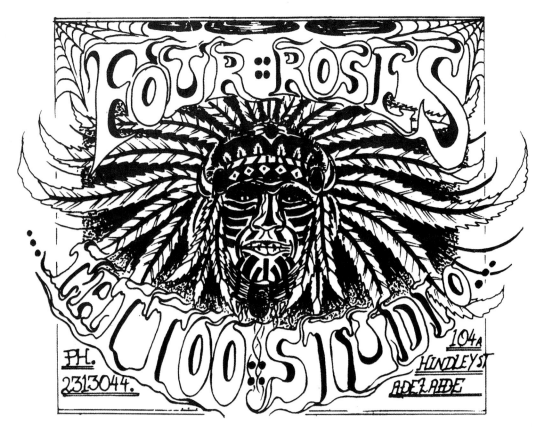

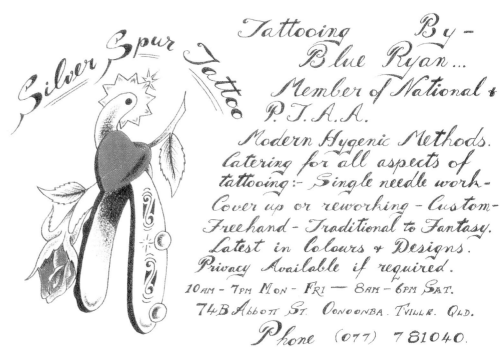
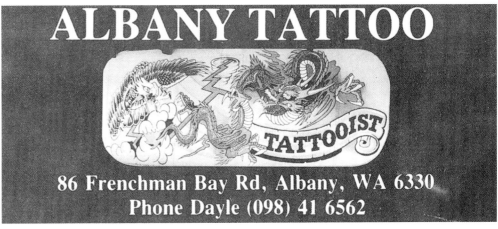

Bicentennial Tattoo

Designed by

Spider Webb

President

Tattoo Club of America

Headquarters

112 West First Street

Mount Vernon, New York 10550

This hand colored and signed print is number ___1086___

of a limited edition of two thousand five hundred

Items like this special United States of America Bicentennial Tattoo Eagle are unusual, but do appear from time to time to commemorate special events.

"TATTOO 78"
......
AMSTERDAM......

"One's enthusiasm
about something
(even tattooing)
doubles and triples,
as one's understanding
of it deepens!"

JOHNNY-TWO-THUMB

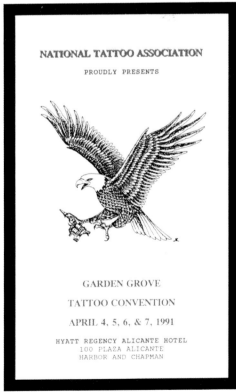

NATIONAL TATTOO ASSOCIATION

PROUDLY PRESENTS

GARDEN GROVE

TATTOO CONVENTION

APRIL 4, 5, 6, & 7, 1991

HYATT REGENCY ALICANTE HOTEL
100 PLAZA ALICANTE
HARBOR AND CHAPMAN

You are invited to
THE FIRST ANNUAL TATTOO BALL
presenting
The Tattoo Revue Show
with live music + dancing

NICK GRAVENITES TRIO
ANNA RIZZO with
  PEE WEE ELLIS BAND

MARK NAFTALIN

SNOOKY FLOWERS

March 31, 1978 8:00pm
Bimbo's 365 Club
1025 Columbus Avenue
San Francisco

$7 per person
Proceeds to Tattoo Art Museum
For tickets call (415) 864-9798 or 641-0526

Dress Fantastic
Valet parking available

Unlike the material which can be acquired by mail order this type of memorabilia can only be gained by attending the actual events and are thus true mementos of things you have experienced.

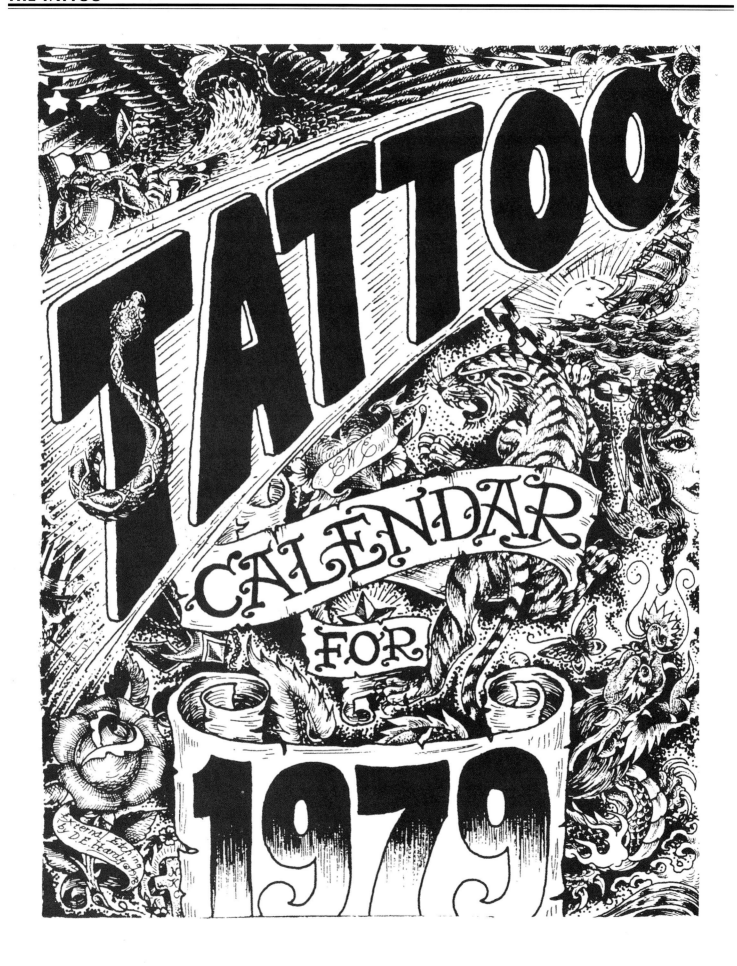

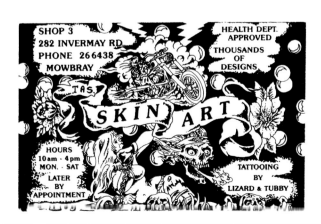

(Left) Painted Lady by American artist Ed Paschke, painted in 1971. (Above) Nueve York, 1971.

Tattoo Wisdom

If you've ever wanted some practical advice about tattooing – apart from "don't do it" - it's hard
to know where to turn. Friends who have tattoos and tattooists may be a little biased.
Your doctor would probably be horrified and forget about asking your mother.
Help is at hand. This section looks at the advantages and disadvantages in
an unbiased way and may help you reach a decision.

Probably as least part of the reason you are reading this book is that, like a great many people, you are fascinated by the tattooist's art. Perhaps that interest will remain an observer's interest, and you may be content to choose to keep your own skin unadorned. That's fine – it is a matter of individual choice and you have the inalienable right to stick to your own decision, free from the influence of anybody else.conversely, you may also have decided - again as a matter of personal choice - to acquire a tattoo. That's fine too. It may be your first tattoo, it may be a subsequent tattoo, it may be for cosmetic considerations, it may be to express something which you feel is important to yourself - personal reasons are as varied and individual as people themselves. The only difference between this decision and any other is that it is largely unalterable, and so only the validity for your decision must come from within yourself. That is not to say that your decision needs to be uninformed - plenty of advice is available. Talk to people: your family, your friends and anybody you know who has made or rejected the same choice. The fact that you have shown yourself capable of thinking something through and arriving at a decision, will mean that the decision you finally take will be respected by everybody as a valid choice.

Once you are committed to having a tattoo, there are certain questions you should ask yourself - and be prepared to answer with total honesty. These are the vital yet fundamental questions of: Why?, How?, Where?, What?, and Who?

Obviously, the first question you must answer is WHY you wish to become tattooed. This is an area where peoples' responses diverge sharply: some acquire a tattoo to conform, while others do the same thing to express their individuality. Either reason may be valid - because some people are naturally gregarious and need to become an accepted member of a group, while others are so individual that they wish to stand apart from groups and declare themselves as being different to others. Only you know your own true inner feelings, so make your decision in the light of informed self-knowledge.

The next question is HOW you wish to be tattooed. This will determine the final result as well as such factors as the

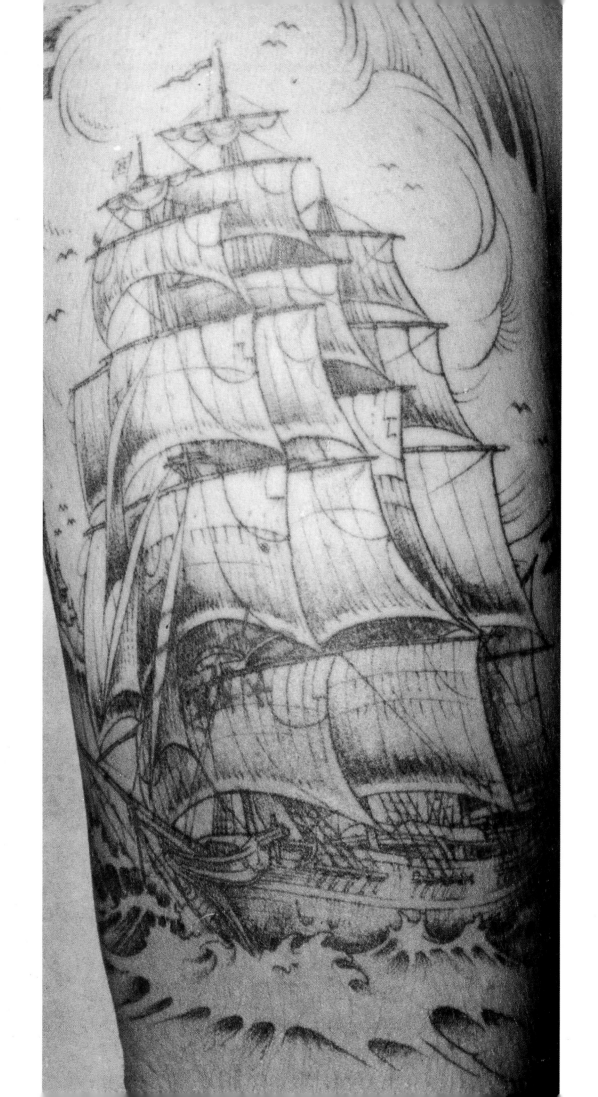

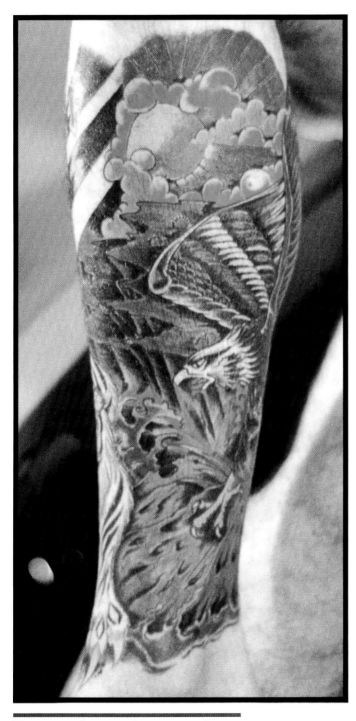

Placement of a tattoo is as personal as the design itself. Some people elect to flaunt it, others to cover it up - as with the professional showpeople who stopped at the neck and wrists, enabling them to cover their tattoos with conventional clothes.
Selecting the site is, to a large extent, dependent upon the design - large pieces are suited to the back or chest. Those like the snake (right) lend themselves to the leg, or arm as the rounded surfaces are an integral part of the design.

time and cost involved in the tattoo or tattoos chosen. You may choose to have a small tattoo, you may wish to have a large tattoo such as a sleeve or full back tattoo, or you may wish to obtain several tattoos from several sources. In a sense, you are choosing the philosophy underlying your choice to become tattooed.

Some people may simply wish to experience the process of tattooing and then living with the result. For them, a small tattoo - whether 'customised' or chosen from a catalogue of 'standard' designs - would probably suffice. For these people, the placement of WHERE the tattoo is to go is likely to be important, for there may be times when they wish to conceal it - whilst with older-fashioned family members or working in an office, for instance. Others choosing a single small design may use it as an accent - a means of highlighting and drawing attention to a particular features such as a curvaceous calf, a shapely shoulder, or perhaps a cleavage.

1940's design by Sailor Jerry Collins.

Design by Ben Corday circa 1920.

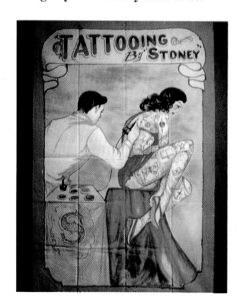

*Tattoos by Stoney 1930 - 40,
by American painter
Fred. G. Johnson.*

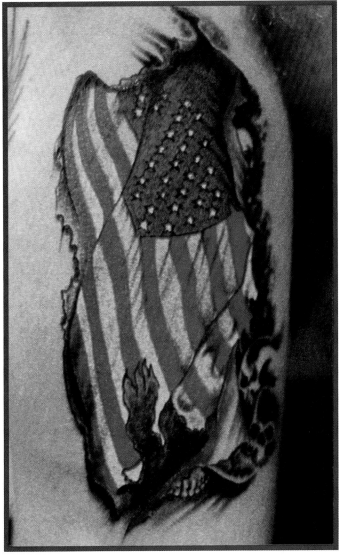

Some people choose to become tattoo collectors. Each design may be an important and permanent 'souvenir' of a particular place, person or period in their lives. For others, having an example of the art of several renowned tattooists, possibly representative of distinct styles, is very important. Such people, while very interested in the specific designs are unlikely to be terribly concerned with the overall aesthetic effect they achieve, simply because it is highly improbable that a complete and unified design will result from a piecemeal process. Some attempts at balancing the areas and density of tattooing are possible and are usually seen as desirable, but a truly integrated overall design is not really practical.

Yet other people may choose large, integrated decorative and often very detailed designs, usually illustrative of some aspect of their particular character. These designs are frequently nostalgic, patriotic, defiant, wistful or simply a sophisticated piece of decoration. This type of tattoo seems to be a current trend, for often such designs win most notice at tattoo showings and competitions.

Whichever path you choose to follow, be aware that tattoos come in three types: the good, the bad and the ugly! The good are those that you find satisfying in every respect and continue to please you throughout your life. The bad are those that don't do that - even though they may be technically perfect and professionally applied. The ugly - and usually they are very ugly indeed - are often 'do-it-yourself' jobs or have been applied by somebody lacking in training and experience. Some are ugly in both subject matter and execution and become a hated stigma during a later period in life. Be wise and make every possible effort to ensure your own tattoo falls into the first category.

The questions of Why? How? and Where? are fairly simple to find your own particular answer to, but the question of What? and Who? are somewhat more difficult because they tend to be interrelated. These are the closely linked areas of choice of design and the choice of tattooist, and since it is true that all tattooists are not created equal in terms of their design abilities, the two are inextricably linked and to a certain degree at least, are interdependent. However, it is also true that a good professional tattooist should be able to meet the design requirements of any client - even if it is only in the competent execution of somebody else's design.

Firstly, it is vital to realise that if your tattoo is to fall into the 'good' category, you must choose a professional tattooist and be prepared to pay accordingly in terms of both time and money. Because of the permanency of your purchase, the tattooists skill should weigh more heavily in your final decision than cost. Indeed, if you are really serious about getting the best possible tattoo, you may even consider the time and cost of travelling interstate or overseas to be justified. This is an extreme example, of course, because

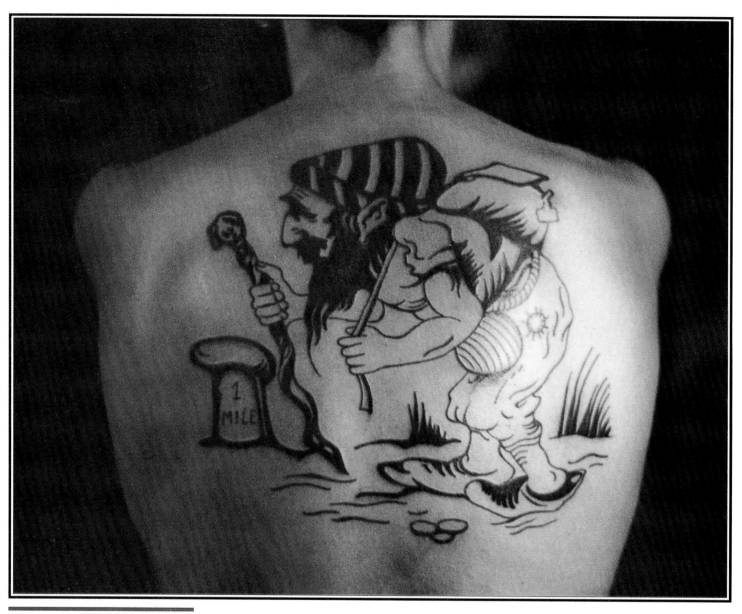

"Going home" by Tony Cohen.

of time and cost are defined constraints for most people, but it illustrates that the choice of tattooist is an important one.

Let us therefore simplify the matter by examining the requirements a client has of a tattoo practitioner.

Firstly, to really be a professional, a tattooist needs to have been trained and to have amassed considerable work experience. Do not hesitate to ask your tattooist about these things, because a reputable tattooist will not take offence at being asked to reassure you by validating their professional claims. He or she will probably be able to show you clear and detailed photographs of past work, may have won trophies and be willing to show them to you, and should certainly be willing to provide you with references which can be checked out independently. If they can't it may be wise to choose somebody else.

Secondly, a professional tattooist will be very conscious of the need for hygiene. The premises clean, sterilisers for equipment evident, rubber gloves will be worn and probably there will be antiseptics and dressings available to treat the tattooed area after a working session. You may be asked to bathe the area to be worked on, or prepare it in some other way if there is any evidence of pimples or some other minor skin disorder.

You may also be asked about any allergies you may have, for some inks may - only very occasionally - produce an adverse bodily reaction. Again, it is wise to listen to any advice your tattooist may offer. If you are at all unsure, ask about these things, and have them explained in detail.

Time is another factor, as is your own individual tolerance of minor pain. Be prepared to be flexible and work in with

NOTICE

This studio is registered with the N.S.W. Association of Professional Tattooists, and as such, is bound by The following rules & regulations.

- The Studio is Operated to the strictest Standard of hygiene, to ensure your safety.
- No Person will be tattooed without Proof of age and identity – You must be 18.
- Persons under 18, but over 16 must complete the statutory declaration, to be signed by a Justice of the Peace. This applies also to Persons already Tattooed if under 18 years.
- No female Person under 18 will be tattooed under any circumstances.
- No Person will be tattooed on the face, hands, neck or feet.
- No female will be tattooed on the exposed parts of the body, which include the arms and lower legs.
- For Persons 16 years to 18 years, the Statutory declaration will be nescessary for each tattoo.
- The consuming of alcohol in or about the studio is strictly forbidden.

THESE REGULATIONS WERE FORMED IN YOUR INTEREST. AND WILL BE STRICTLY ADHERED TO IN ALL REPUTABLE N.S.W. TATTOO STUDIOS. A TATTOO IS A PERMANENT FORM OF ADORNMENT. THESE RULES WERE DESIGNED TO ENSURE THAT YOU WILL BE HAPPY WITH YOUR DECISION TO BECOME TATTOOED. THANK YOU FOR YOUR CUSTOM AND CO-OPERATION!

YOUR ARTIST ———

Members of the New South Wales Association of Professional Tattooists won't do this. But obviously there are tattooists who will. In the event, think carefully before you have it done. You need to be pretty dedicated to tattooing to commit youself this far.

your tattooist in arranging mutually suitable session times. Very small tattoos can be completed in a single session, but larger works do take time to complete. Realise that during the process of tattooing, two people are involved, and either may become fatigued. In the matter of pain, although it may be slight, be aware that it can be stressful, and may influence your attitudes or judgement. Never permit yourself to become overly tense or sore simply for the sake of continuing - there is always another time. A good tattooist understands these things, so discuss them openly if the need to do so arises.

Professional practitioners are patient people who realise the permanence and significance of a tattoo. They will be ready to discuss your specific design requirements patiently and in detail. They will seek to reach a full understanding of matters such as overall design or effect, placement, techniques, colours and any lettering - before they commence work. Be prepared to listen to them, because their advice may be invaluable - and is part of the skill and experience you are paying for. Equally, if something they suggest for your tattoo is definitely not what you want, speak out clearly, and make your objections known. You are the one who decides what may and may not be done and you are the one who must live with the result - in this regard the tattooist is only the means to the end result.

Finally, there is the matter of design - the most personal and significant aspect of it all if you are to remain satisfied with your tattoo for years still to come. Nobody can dictate what you will consider is good - but they will discuss it. The most important discussion about it will obviously be the one with your own tattooist. A competent and professional practitioner may inform you about possibilities and limitations - but they cannot decide what you like. Unless you are prepared to accept a tattooist by their design reputation alone and place yourself entirely in their hands, or are prepared to accept a 'standardised' catalogue design, get yourself informed!

You can do this by observing other peoples' tattoos and by reading extensively among the many magazines devoted to the tattoo art. You may even wish to attend tattoo competitions and discuss the matter with the people there. Let your own aesthetic tastes range widely, develop and firm – and then trust your own judgement!

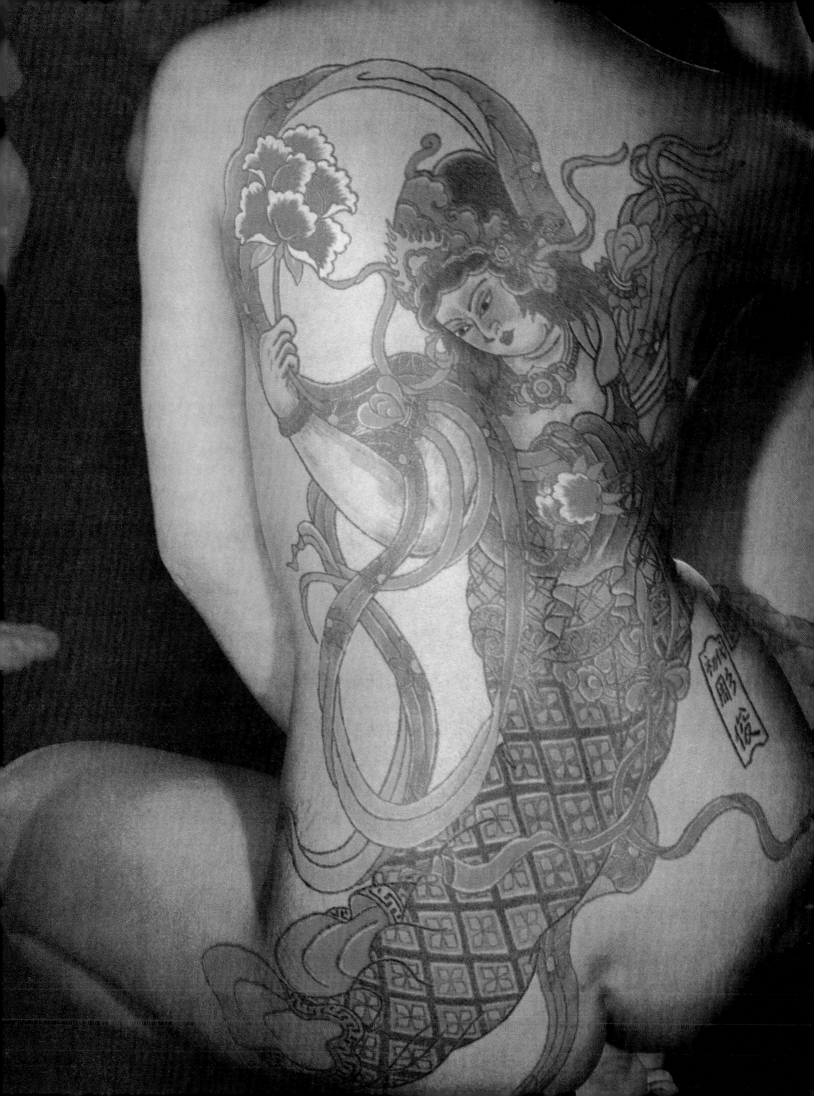

PiERCE dE RESiSTANCE

Putting holes in the body for decorative purposes is probably as old as tattooing. Indeed in one form – ear piercing – has gained such widespread acceptance that women who do not have their ears pierced are probably in the minority. But beyond this, body piercing is a fringe activity and one which does appear to have quite a number of drawbacks, although enthusiasts claim that the advantages far outweigh the disadvantages.

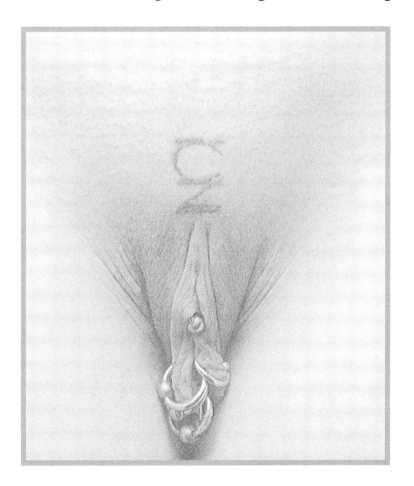

A practice frequently seen used in association with tattooing is that of body piercing - the insertion of studs or rings, usually fashioned of metal, into holes pierced through the flesh. The inserted object is left within the flesh while healing occurs to prevent the hole from sealing completely. The hole is made only for the purpose of attaching some adornment in a firm and convenient manner.

Such holes are not always truly permanent, as they may eventually close up if not kept open by an insert, but they generally last quite a long time. Provided that something is inserted permanently, or sufficiently frequently, the hole remains. The most commonly found instance is the piercing of the lobes of the ears in order to attach earrings, a practice

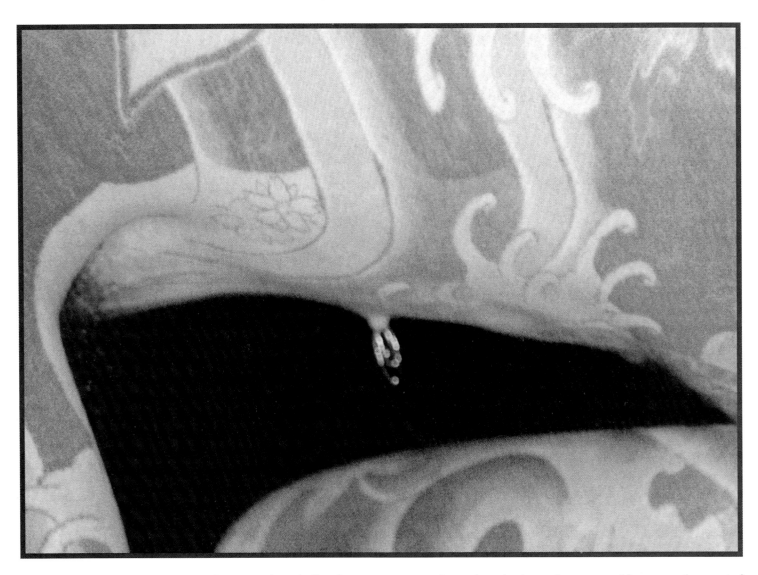

which has been followed by fashion-conscious ladies for many years.

Commonly, the ear lobe is numbed by the application of ice or a localised anaesthetic agent applied to the skin, then pierced by a sterilised needle. An antiseptic is applied, a smooth metallic stud is inserted and the ear lobe is allowed to heal naturally. Once this has occurred, the stud may be removed and reinserted without undue pain, and provided normal hygiene is maintained and no dirt is allowed to accumulate within the hole, the piercing will no longer present any significant risk of infection.

It is important to note that the object inserted must be smooth to prevent it sticking as healing takes place, or becoming abrasive later, and it must be of a safe substance. For these reasons the insert is generally of metal, either stainless steel, or one of the most acid-resistant noble metals of gold or silver. The use of other and baser metals is dangerous – they can be attacked by substances within the bloodstream or by other substances secreted through the skin, with the results of disfiguring marking becoming evident or toxic reactions beginning. It is also important to note that unless the insert is a removable one such as a stud or an open ring, it becomes permanently attached. Closed rings are an example of where this applies.

Increasingly, body piercing is becoming common in places other than in the earlobes, and more frequently with closed and thus permanent inserts. Some people are now having their upper ears, nasal septums, nipples, and sometimes even their genitalia, pierced and fitted with metal rings. Often the rings alone are deemed sufficient ornament, but sometimes they are also used to support further adornments such as chains or other freely dangling attachments.

While the right of the individual to use or adorn their own body in any way they wish is undeniable, the wisdom of some of these instances of body piercing is open to serious questioning. This is because in the most extreme cases it is disturbingly close to a phenomenon universally recognised as a psychological aberration - the practice of deliberate self-mutilation. Of course, this is largely an argument of degree and of function: nobody would seriously question the practicality of ear piercing to accommodate earrings – but what of pierced nipples with permanently attached

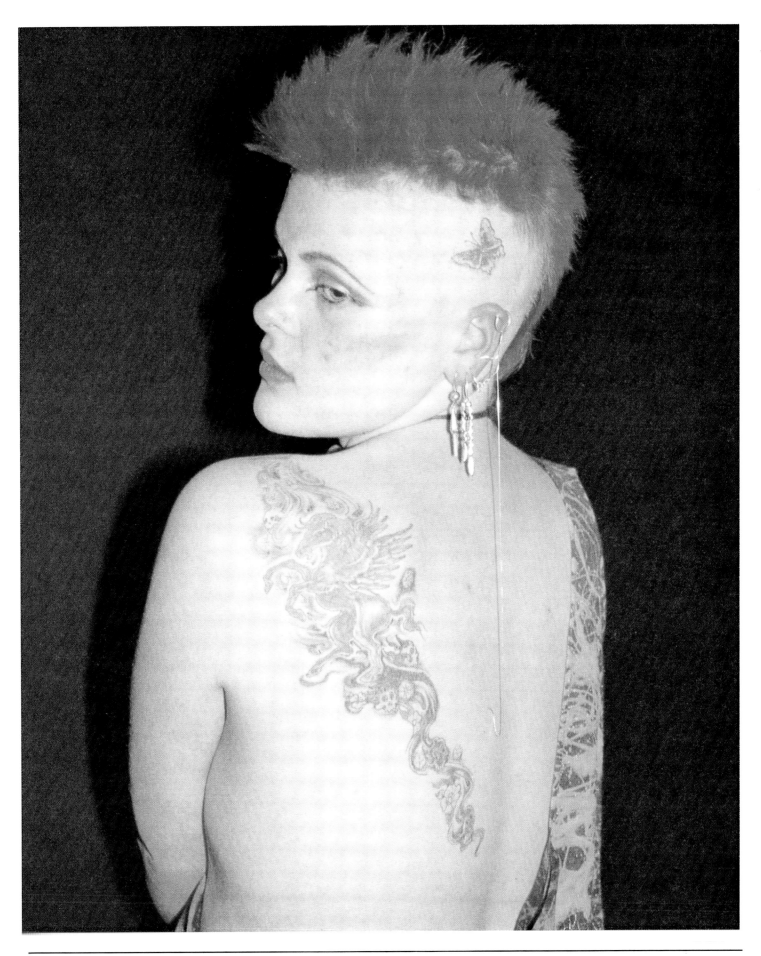

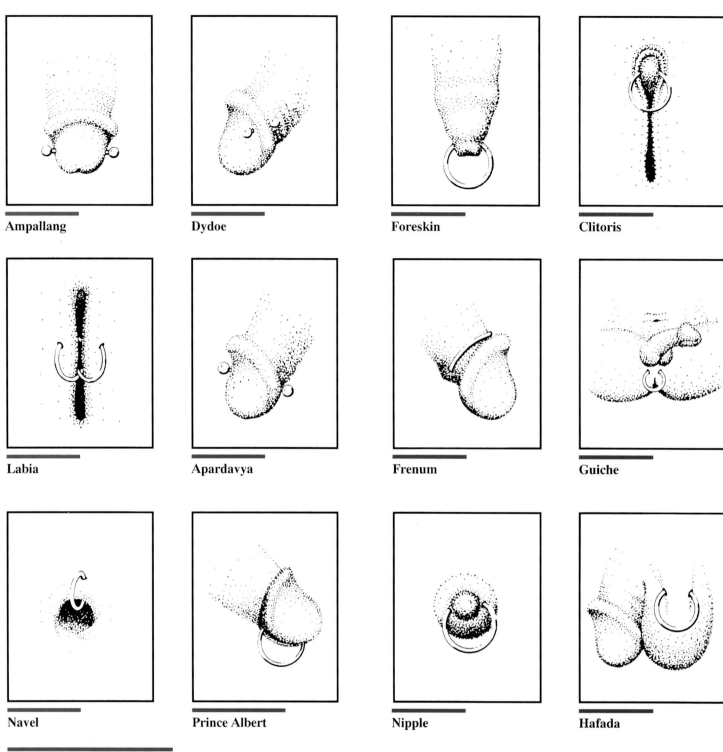

Ampallang Dydoe Foreskin Clitoris

Labia Apardavya Frenum Guiche

Navel Prince Albert Nipple Hafada

These diagrams illustrate the most common forms of non-facial body piercings - mostly of the genitals.

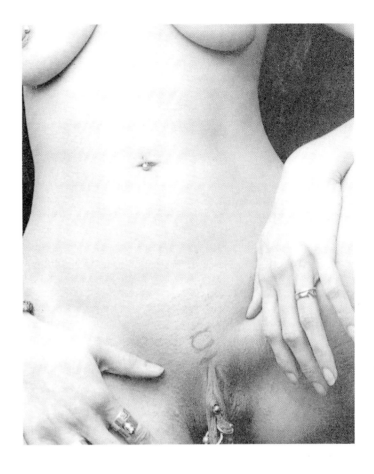

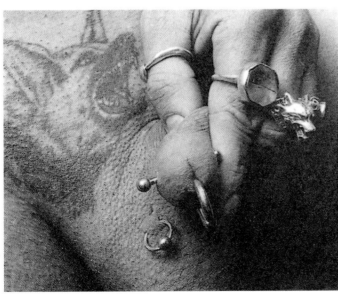

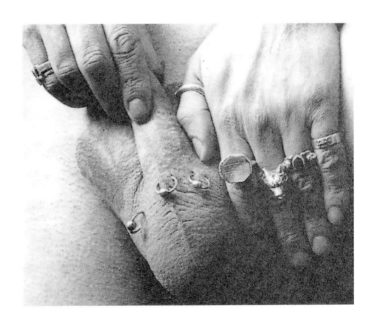

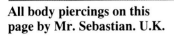

All body piercings on this page by Mr. Sebastian. U.K.

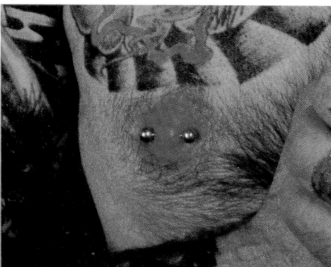

metal rings on a lactating new mother, or a penis so pierced and densely covered with metal rings that it appeared to be clad in chain mail? Instances of both of the latter examples have been recorded, and provide cases of adornment being taken to such lengths that it interferes with natural function. Most reasonable members of society would consider these, admittedly rare and extreme cases very 'sick'. and few people could condone them. Clearly practicality should be evident, and commonsense should prevail.

The purpose of both body piercing and tattooing is adornment and a declaration of individuality, so it is fair to compare the two practices. Both have certain advantages and disadvantages worthy of consideration.

Undoubtedly, the addition of metal to the flesh can produce a sharper and more intensely reflective gleam than tattoos can, and so it may be valid to use a metal adornment as an accent point to highlight a particular area of skin, whether that area is tattooed or not. Rings pierced through flesh can also be used to attach chains or some form of pendant, and so can add a rapid and possibly sparkling movement to an overall appearance; an effect impossible to achieve with the slower movements of muscle. Unlike a tattoo, a stud or anything attached to a ring is temporary, and may be changed at will. This is undeniably an advantage - try hanging something from a tattoo! However, the question remains as to whether or not a similar range of effects – metallic gleam and rapid movement – is not better achieved by more conventional jewellery such as neck chains, armlets and the like.

So what are some of the disadvantages of body piercing inserts? Let's deal with the practicalities first. There are remarkably few sites on the human body where the flesh is sufficiently thin or protuberant to pierce right through: only the nostrils, nasal septum, ears, nipples, tongue, lips, cheeks and possibly some parts of the genitalia – all rather small in extent. Clearly, those areas where muscle tissue is involved in significant movement, and lies just beneath the skin, are impractical because any insert would constantly cause tearing of the skin and possibly the muscle fibres themselves. We can rule out some of the above sites too. Permanent decoration of the genitalia is rather pointless unless we live our lives in a state of nudity, the flesh in the groin area is particularly sensitive and remains so because of constant perspiring. Further, because of the proximity of the excretory functions any piercing of the skin is particularly susceptible to becoming infected. The cheeks, lips and tongue are unsuitable sites for similar reasons: any piercing is likely to be coated with food particles, and natural decomposition of these will ensure that the piercing will quickly become a site of infection. Additionally, there might be unsightly leakage of saliva or other fluids – depending on the site of the hole. This leaves the nose, ears and nipples.

Fortunately, all of these small areas are well protected as we move about in out daily lives. Which is just as well – studs are never truly firmly fixed, and so are easily lost if

something inadvertently catches upon them. This is not so with permanently embedded rings. If they catch upon something and the impetus of our body weight is sufficient, the flesh will tear before the ring breaks. Painful and unsightly injury can result. Considering all of these points, we can only conclude that in many instances body piercing is impractical. By way of contrast, tattooing has none of these disadvantages.

But we have strayed from the point: the purpose of body piercing is assumed to be adornment and individuality. Again, it does not stack up very well: the curvature of the body surfaces severely limits the size of studs, and this in turn limits their design and so, their visual impact. Embedded rings have similar limitations – the cross sectional diameter being one, and the need to have uniform curves and so sharp corners being another. Weight and length are limits which restrict the design of anything which is hung from them. All these restrictions tend to make most body piercing inserts fairly uniform in appearance and visual effect – so largely defeating any quest for individuality.

Perhaps though, the most damning design factor is that all body piercing inserts are externalised - they are never perceived as truly being part of the person who wears them. This is because they must always fall outside of the human silhouette, and we are so totally accustomed to this shape that anything that does not conform to it is always seen as an addition, rather than an integral part. There seems to be an idea deeply embedded within the human psyche that our individuality, other than our own characteristic behaviour, extends from within ourselves and outwards to our skin - and no further. In this regard alone, an insert which becomes an external break in the smooth shape of the human anatomy. Again, by way of contrast, tattoos suffer from none of these constraints.

Doubtless, ear and nipple piercing are here to stay. Equally doubtless, if you decide to adopt them it is far better to have them properly performed by somebody such as a tattooist, who is aware of all of the practical design and hygiene considerations, that it is to attempt them yourself. But they have a limited role to play in bodily decoration.

Meditations

While THE TATTOO is a celebration of the art and beauty of tattooing, there are other facets which we'll look at briefly. There are a number of medical considerations to be aware of before having a tattoo. There are also problems associated with the complete removal of tattoos.

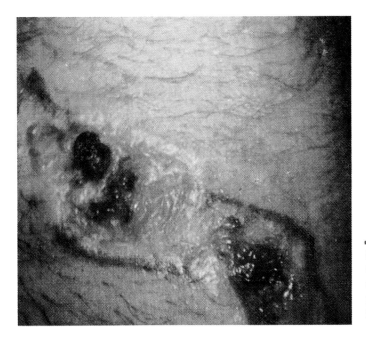

(Left) A reaction on a tattoo, while uncommon does show what can happen when things go wrong with tattooing.

Dr. Andrew Lemes of Hollywood, California, some years ago investigated the toxicity of pigments used in the tattoo process, comparing modern colours with those used in the past. Here are his comments,

Now tattooists can buy colours more economically wholesale and can avoid potentially harmful pigments. It should be noted than **chromates** or chromium-containing compounds are carcinogenic and must be avoided. Do not use the chrome-plated tubes for tattoo machines. Use only stainless steel tubes. Use ceramic ball tumbler (available from lapidary suppliers) to grind pigments finer - e.g. Dalamar yellow - for brighter colours.

Lead poisoning is cumulative, so those of you who plan large work should be certain that the needle-bars are soldered with 90% tin - 10% silver plumbers' solder, **not** 60 - 40% lead solder. As the soldered needles go in and out of the "pigment well" they may dissolve out lead.

The next section describes toxicity studies of currently used tattoo pigments. Generally, **worry ye not**, rat studies indicate extremely low toxicity levels. You could ingest 454 grams of most pigments without toxic effects. The next section deals with white tattoo that are almost invisible (T_1O_2) unless one gets into a sauna or hot-tub and toxicity studies of pigments.

Toxicity Studies of Pigments Currently Used in Tattooing: Previously discussed were pigments used for intradermal deposition in the tattooing process. In the 1950's Jerry Collins, an innovative master of the Japanese-

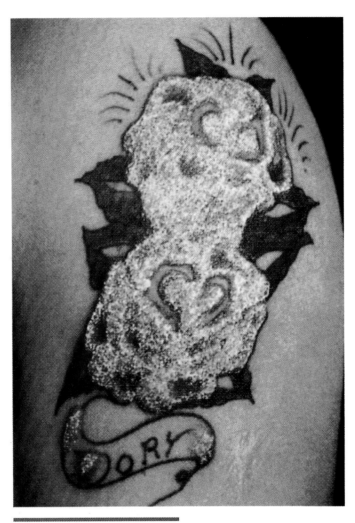

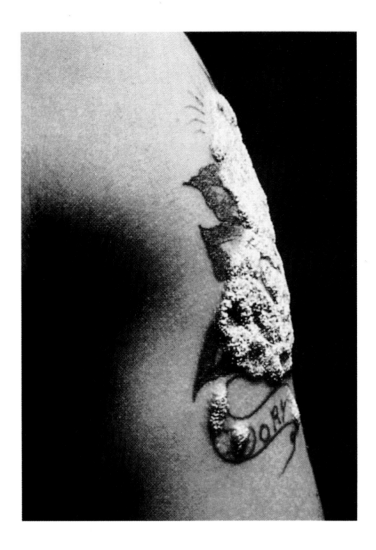

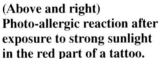

(Above and right)
**Photo-allergic reaction after
exposure to strong sunlight
in the red part of a tattoo.**

style of tattooing from Honolulu, Hawaii, introduced some new and stronger tattooing pigments. One was a pigment used in the paint industry produced an intense which did not deposit unevenly in the skin. It was composed of 87% Azo-pigment (yellow), 7% calcium resinate, and 5% barium sulfate. When fed orally to 10 rats, the L.D. 50 was greater than 20 grams per kilogram. (L.D. 50 refers to the lethal dose at which greater than 50% of the test animals die after ingestion of a compound being tested for toxicity. Extrapolated to a 70 kilogram adult male, he would have to eat over 1.4 kilograms of the substance of this yellow to be harmful to the extent of inducing death in over 50% of those ingesting it, probably. That means that it is "safer than salt" according to a toxicologist doctor consulted by the author.

The rare purple or violet pigment given to a select few of the tattooing world 20 years ago was Doxime Carbazole, used in photographic plate production and as a paint pigment. According to toxicology tests and the Poison Control Centre of Los Angeles, carbazole compounds can be allergy provoking (or an allergen). Toxicity studies in rats indicate an L.D. 50 of greater than 5 grams per kilogram or 350 gram of pigment for a 70 kilogram man. Carbazole is an extremely weak base and very insoluble in water. When in the skin, it would be a water-based system and thus very insoluble. It again is "safer than salt" when eaten. No one tattooed with this substance to our knowledge has had an allergic reaction to it.

The beautiful vivid blues and permanent greens of present day tattooing are the copper phthalocyanine compounds, which are **not** at all related to "the cyanides". They are used in Grumbacher artists' paints and in the printing industry. According to Dr. George Stevenson, an industrial toxicologist, they are very inert and can be considered like carbon particles. Copper phthalocyanine is a copper complex of less than 10% copper by molecular weight. Solubility in water systems, such as human skin tissue is very poor. L.D. 50 for copper phthalocyanine blue is greater than 10 grams per kilogram in the rat test animal, which means a lethal dose for the 70 kilogram male human would be over 700 grams. The phthalocyanine blue may cause a slight swelling

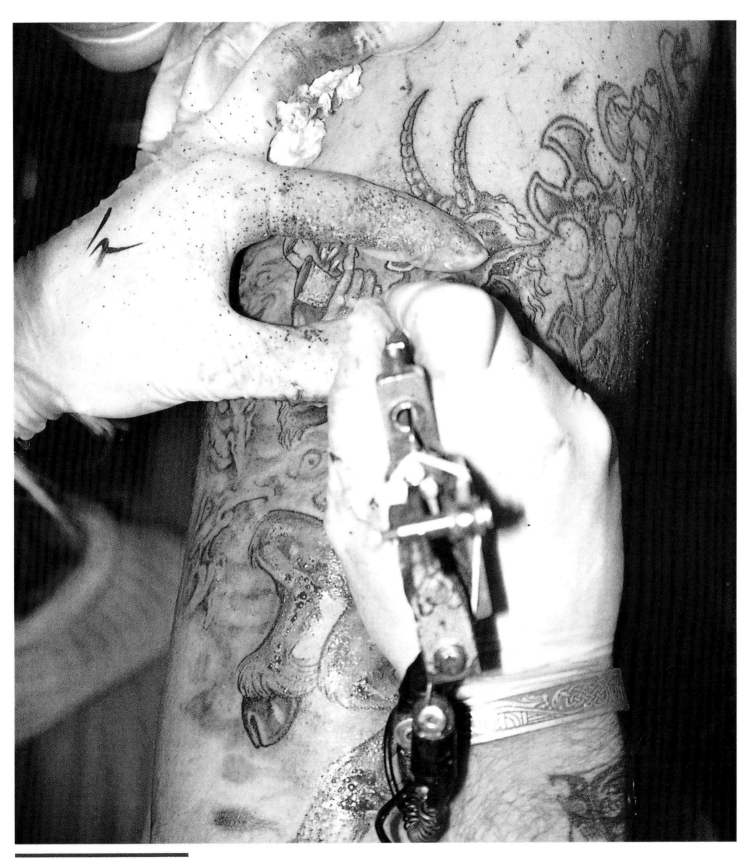

To minimise the risk of
infection, reputable tattooists
insist on the highest standards
of hygiene.

**All equipment should appear
well cared for, not showing
signs of neglect such as rust.**

or intradermal oedema of the skin after exposure of an area tattooed with it to bright sunlight over an extended period of time. The itching and swelling are transient and just last several days, if a large dose of sunlight is received.

The last pigment to be discussed is white. It has an extremely fascinating history in that it has been used in Japan in the 19th century for a particular type of "invisible" tattooing. Beautiful designs such as that of a white fox could be tattooed on a person's back and would only be seen or would develop if the person went into a hot sauna or bath. The superficial capillaries in the skin would dilate in the hot sauna which would make the person's skin blush or redden. The white lines of the tattoo would then become visible against the reddened background of skin. The effect has been relatively unknown among tattooists today.

The Japanese at first used the highly toxic white lead, **lead oxide**, to produce the white tattoo. The tattooing caused the symptoms of lead poisoning among the tattooees. Zinc oxide then replaced the lead oxide as less toxic. Finally, the extremely intense artists' colour of **titanium dioxide** (white) replaced both. Titanium white is stable, highly opaque and non-toxic as far as this author had been able to find. It is an inert, harmless compound found in the best artists' paints such as Grumbacher's. The maxim of the tattooists prior to the advent of T_1O_2 was that nothing could cover carbon black. For that matter some of the phthalocyanine blues or greens (from DuPont) can not be used for outlining designs so intense are they.

Japanese Techniques:

In Japan, as opposed to the case of early America, the human skin or epidermis was regarded as a canvas when it came to the subject of tattooing. It was similar in concept to the mid-nineteenth century *niskiki-e* or brocade woodblock prints. Western tattooing was considered ornamental on light skin; whereas Japanese tattooing was distinguished by a dark background from which designs appeared by contrast - a *chiaroscuro* effect. Japanese fog or *sfumato* was also used to produce swirling areas of grey or darkness. *Beta* was a Japanese term which meant to paint the skin thickly and the term *bokashi* referred to various shadings of darkness.

If stencils are used they must be cleaned between each use to reduce the risk of hepatitis

Japanese tattoo technique consisted of using capillarity between adjacent tattooing needles to facilitate absorption of the injected pigments.

(In the West recently the need for two or three needles has been eliminated by using a cluster of three needles with the central needle protruding by 7mm beyond the tips of the other two #12 needles. Only the central needle penetrated the skin, but the two adjacent needles added to the capillary effect needed to ink the central tattooing needle). This was called "one needle outlining" and had previously only been used in the context of the prison environment where prisoners pricked designs into their skins using a guitar string as a needle. The one needle effect gave an extremely fine line and appeared like a burin engraving.

In Japan, delicate designs were accomplished but nothing so fine as in one needle outlining. The Japanese were more concerned with large designs and used clusters or groupings of many needles to accomplish these. Japanese tattoo needles, which apparently started as slivers of bamboo possibly, were placed in rows of five until a maximum of 40 were bundled into a circular-bunch shape.

Recent Japanese tattooists have been using century-old designs, but they have switched to Western electric tattoo machines for ease and speed of application.

The old technique, before the advent on the Japanese scene of electric machines required a fine and rhythmic wrist action. Needles were applied to a taut skin in a lever fashion with the thumb of the left hand acting as a fulcrum.

Two Japanese needle techniques were: *Hanebari* for producing black space and *Imo-tsuki* for cuttingdelicate designs.

The main pigments used in pre-World War II days were: brown, vermilion and sumi (black, carbon ink block). The mercury substance of the vermilion red caused a high fever and mercuric poisoning. The fever which occurred from vermilion tattooing was sometimes used to treat syphilis, as most syphilis agents, or spirochaetes were killed by a high fever of the host organism, sometimes. New, less toxic, pigments were imported from Australia and the traditional black and white Chinese painting approach to tattooing declined.

Oshiroi-bori meant a white tattoo that emerged into view upon the skin when one was slightly intoxicated. The skin turned pink from the superficial blood vessel dilation due to the effect of the alcohol and the white tattoo contrasted delicately with the pink skin colour.

This technique has been tried in at least one Western case. A snowflake was tattooed in white on the forearm using

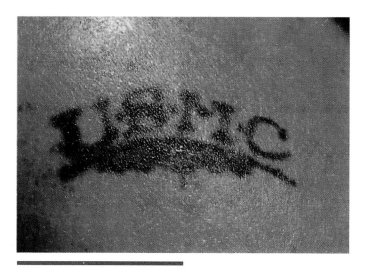

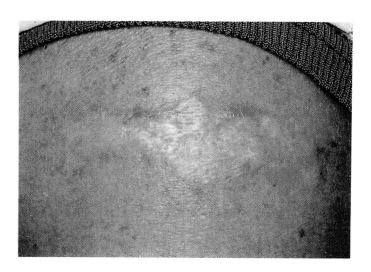

(Above left) A tattoo before removal and (above right) the scarring that resulted from its removal by an abrasive method.

titanium oxide pigment. Originally lead was used (lead oxide) for the white tattoos and was highly toxic until the introduction of non-toxic titanium oxide white pigment.

Solutions Used To Suspend Tattooing Pigments:

Historically for 50 years, Listerine (an American mouthwash) was used by tattooists to suspend the pigments used to tattoo. Before the recent reformulation of Listerine, it contained a small amount to phenol, or carbolic acid, which is a potent bacteriostatic agent. Other components of Listerine acted as wetting agents to keep the pigment particles wet so that they would stick to the tattooist's needles and be conveyed into the skin. The wetting agent's primary function was to keep insoluble pigment particles suspended in a vehicle which was innocuous to the skin. Unfortunately, phenol can be irritating. Other times, an allergy was said by some tattooists to occur to Listerine as it contains a number of other ingredients not really formulated to be injected into the skin. Glycerine (just a few drops) could be used to prevent drying out of the colour jars and as an emulsifying agent.

Currently, the best tattooists formulate colours in this way: Dry D & C approved coloured pigments (which have been ground fine in a ceramic ball tumbler or with mortar and pestle) are mixed with pure 70% isopropyl alcohol (easily obtainable rubbing alcohol without any added ingredients such as methyl salicylate or menthol). Several drops of pure glycerine are added by some artists at this point (others use Rosewater and glycerine in equal parts). Put the mixture into a blender (such as a Waring Blender), blend well into a **very heavy creamlike consistency.** Sterile, distilled, water may be added later for thinning for "water-colour" wash effects if needed, at a later point when actually executing the tattooing process. The mixture is then put into Pyrex glass containers, such as baby bottles, and autoclaved

to destroy bacteria and hepatitis virions or virus particles (some pigments might be affected by autoclaving). Teflon, autoclave labware is used by some of the best tattoo artists. According to one study, pigment particle size should be around six micra. Pigment milling information may or may not be available. Food grade T_1O_2 is very finely milled and "works" better.

Current Tattooing Techniques & Methods:

Many artists of today have used self-closing, plastic 114ml and 226ml polyethylene or autoclavable plastic Teflon bottles to contain the prepared, cream-like pigment formulations. These may be arranged in an array like an artist's palette. so that individual amounts of the creamy pigment paste can be placed in sterile polyethylene cups containing about two or three cc. In this way, each of the artist's clients gets uncontaminated and separate pigment pots, which are thrown away after use. Distilled water or alcohol can be used to dilute the pigments for various shading effects, such as "Sumi water shading" which entails tattooing with a very dilute solution of black tattooing ink. The result is a fogging effect on the skin similar to a water colour "wash". The effect has been called *sfumato*, which means fog in Japan. Japanese tattooists have, of course, used a bar of carbon-based ink in the past for calligraphy. The technique of the ink block was called "Sumi".

To prepare the canvas or skin for tattooing, the area to be tattooed is shaved with an individual disposable razor. It is impossible to sterilise the skin surface, as the normal skin bacteria or flora permeates the depth of the epidermis or dead-cell layers to the junction of the living-cell layer or *rete pegs* of the dermis. It is probably best to employ a povidone-iodide solution, such as commercially available Betadine, to disinfect the skin or dermal surface.

Next, the tattoo design is sketched on the prepared area of skin. Some artists take into account the topography of the area in relation to natural skin folds and the underlying muscular masses. If the design is placed upon the skin while the area in question is contorted, distortion may occur when the area goes back to normal or "anatomical" position.

For example, when an "eagle design" is sketched on the chest, the person should be standing upright with arms relaxed at his sides. When the design is placed, then it will appear undistorted in most anatomical positions the person takes. At the same time, changes in skin topography can be used for certain effects. For example, the eagle on the chest can be used to flap its wings if the person wearing it raises his arms over his head. Changes in dermal topography can be studied in *Living Anatomy* by R. D. Lockhart, M.D. (University of Aberdeen) 6th Ed.. 1962. pub: The University Press, Glasgow, Scotland. The skin's remarkable elasticity must be taken into consideration with every tattoo placed.

There have been several methods to place a design on the skin prior to finalising it with the tattoo needle. One old method utilised a clear, acetate or plastic sheet upon which the design to be used was etched using a sharp pointed tool or vibrating engraver's needle. Fine carbon or lampblack was sifted onto the plastic template of the design and the powder would stick to the engraved lines. Then the area of skin to be tattooed was thinly coated with Vaseline or petroleum jelly, from a collapsible tube to prevent contamination of the petroleum jelly. The acetate or plastic stencil was then pushed against the skin and carefully pulled away leaving a thin black carbon outline of the tattoo design. As the carbon particles were easily smeared obscuring the design, better ways were sought to place the design.

The old stencil method just described is still used where "assembly-line" tattoos are done. in old-fashioned tattoo parlours. The design stencils are kept on file for new customers and cleaned with alcohol between uses. Thus, hepatitis virus or bacteria might be passed from one customer to another with this method of "stencil templates".

Other, free-hand artists have employed "Hectograph" pencils to trace their original designs on tracing paper and then transfer the design to the client's skin surface. The Hectograph method produced a non-smearing design upon the skin, and the toxicity of the ink was nil. Other tattoo artists sketched the design on the skin using a sterile toothpick dipped in black tattooing ink, or held in the grip of a mechanical drawing pencil. This as opposed to the Hectograph technique allowed wider artistic expression by the artist drawing directly on the variable contours of the human skin-canvas. However, when the actual messy process of tattooing began; the black ink outline could be easily effaced by blood, serous ooze and splattering tattoo ink.

Methylene blue stain powder when diluted to about 10% or less with alcohol made a good alternative to any other

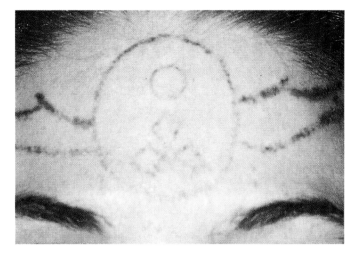

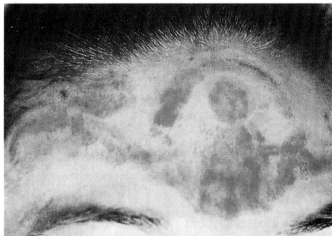

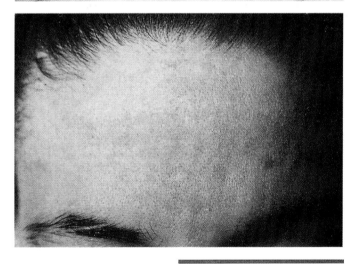

The three photographs (above) show the stages in the removal of a tattoo by demabrasion. It shows less scarring that the previous example.

Painless Jeff Publications, ITAA Convention, Reno 1977

Printed in England at The Manor Press, Deal, Kent

Tattoos and their removal is not all serious – two tattooists look at the lighter side of their profession. (Above) from Jeff Baker of Deal and (left) a cartoon by Hamming.

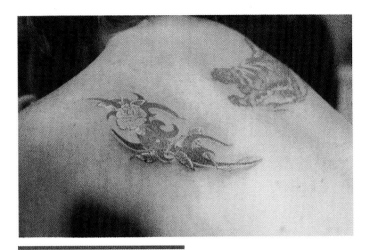

Most people experience transient irritation when tattooed. This soon passes if the tattooists instructions are followed. Ask his advice on how to look after your tattoo until it has healed. It is especially important that the area does not become sunburnt at this time.

method of marking the skin with the design *prior* to the actual finalisation of the outline of the tattoo with the tattoo machine's outliner needles. With methylene blue stain the client wishing the tattoo could "try on" a design for a few days before committing himself to the tattooing operation. With the tattoo design placed on the surface of the skin in a methylene blue stain form, the area to be tattooed could be coated with a thin layer of petroleum jelly. The petroleum prevented splattering from happening when the outlining operation with the tattoo machine began. This technique of outlining the tattoo will now be described in detail.

As before described, the tattoo machine consisted of a reciprocating metal rod (the needle bar) with plated or stainless steel needles soldered to the end (number 12). Plated needles must be checked under a magnifying lens to rule out hooks or bad plating, or use stainless steel #2 Entomology pins. If the needles are not properly dried and stored in mineral oil after autoclaving them in the case of plated needles, they will become corroded and microscopically pitted. Corroded needles do not allow the pigment to flow into the skin as easily as sharp, smooth ones. The skin surface had to be very **taut** when tattooing or nothing good could be accomplished.

Dr Nemes, who is a full-on tattoo enthusiast has also made a study of the criteria by which tattoos should be judged. He splits the subject into twenty sections and for officials judging at shows and conventions will make fascinating reading.

There are many criteria by which tattooing could be judged or compared. This author's study of the subject has suggested about twenty aspects which are enumerated below.

1. *Quality of line* included evenness of line, width, and variability. A fuzzy, crudely executed line could be compared unfavourably to a fine, exact and precisely defined line. Maori *moko* or deep-line tattooing was superbly defined, whereas other primitive tattooing had wider lines due to the instrument utilised. The Japanese hand-method which used as few as one or two sharp needles produced very fine lines. The modern electric tattooing machine, using three to five needles produced an even line in expert hands only, but one which was usually very thick. The "one-needle" technique produced the thinnest line.

2. *Use of value* (the intensity of light) was perfected in the *chiaroscuro* and subtle changes in the centuries of Japanese tattooing. In *chiaroscuro*, figures emerge from a dark background. The figure-ground effect or Gestalt is very important.

3. *Use of Chroma* (the brightness or intensity of colour, its dilution with dark pigment) again was at its acme in Japan where many shades of the same colour were used in this century. Earlier Japanese tattooing employed only a few colours. Few modern tattooists could duplicate the delicate colours of Japanese tattooing until recent pigment developments. If too much colour is injected into an area of a tattoo, pigment overload can occur, which causes a lumpy appearing area.

4. *Use of hue* (the actual range of distinct colours, distinguished by a specific wavelength as determined from reflected or incident light). The Japanese used black (which appeared blue on light transmitted through the skin) and vermilion, (cinnabar) but one report indicated that up to 17 colours had been used. Hori Chiyo, master Japanese tattooist of the 1800s, added brown to the repertoire of the artist. American tattooists of the past, not exactly of the colourist school, limited their colours to blue for outlines and red and green for fill. The old pigments were salts of poisonous metals usually and worked into the skin with difficulty. Brown figured occasionally as did yellow. Unfortunately, dark yellow and red often contained cadmium and mercuric compounds which irritated the skin sometimes long after application. In 1950, still, no good violet (other than a poor manganese compound) existed for most tattooists. Only a few tattooists held the pigment secrets at that time which allowed vibrant hues to be put into the skin. There were, though, many flesh tones and browns available.

5. *Monochromatic or polychromatic* (use of one chroma or many chromas) depended on the effect, as in any artistic endeavour, one wished to achieve against the textured, flesh-tone canvas of the skin. Often, the Japanese used only outlining in one hue as did the amateur. Alternately, the skin-canvas could be "washed" with a background of one

hue. Popularly, "monochromatic" or "polychromatic" meant use of one hue or many hues, but technically as correctly defined in two, three and four.

6. *Changes of level of the skin* were not apparent in the Japanese hand-method or electric tattooing, except for swelling and accentuation of parts of the design on rubbing, or use of a hot-water shower. Keloids (raised scar tissue) might appear on Negroid skin (outside of the face where keloids do not usually form). *Moko,* used by the Maoris, made use of the fact that keloids did not form on the face. They actually dug grooves in the face in a kind of bas relief with the pigment placed at the bottom of the groove. Thus *Moko* was not actually what we consider to be tattooing.

7. *Topographic changes in the skin upon movement* (changes in size of the marked area of skin when the skin is stretched by muscle contraction or movement of a joint) have been taken into account by some American tattooists. Eagles' wings have flapped on the chest as the arms were raised; Hula-hula girls have gyrated as biceps bulged; and verbal saying have been formed when tattooed fingers of either hand have been interdigitated; nude figures have entered into coitus with appropriate movements. Nipples have served as clowns' noses. Tentacles of a squid have undulated on the arms and legs in one large design which emanated from a central back and buttocks area.

8. *Harmony of design placement or arrangement,* like city development, has occurred helter-skelter or by a carefully balanced plan. Some extensively tattooed persons acquired designs with a final plan or goal in mind. Others have compulsively piled-on design after ill-conceived design without regard to the final result. The Japanese were noted for large, panoramic designs which sometimes covered torso, arms, forearms, and lower extremities with one planned creation. The majority of American electric tattooing, unfortunately, has been applied as smaller, non-integrated and non-related designs, with a poor balance in a classical sense. Yet, in a way the kitsch of a scramble of designs can be very attractive.

9. *Use of realism* in a tattooed picture, of course, demanded skill in drawing and knowledge of light, form, colour and perspective on the part of the tattoo-artist. The Japanese excelled in their use of three dimensions, as opposed to flat, two-dimensional quality of most other classes of tattooists. Sutherland MacDonald, an English tattooist of the 1800s and probably the best tattooist studied, had as *his piece de resistance* two eagles locked in combat with feathers flying in perfect detail as a "chest piece" (large tattoo, in tattooists parlance, for the chest). Most American tattooing consisted of traced or stencilled designs, few of which were original or possessed of startling, detailed realism. Ed Hardy (Realistic Tattoo, San Francisco) and Cliff Raven (Sunset Strip Tattoo, Los Angeles) were two pioneers whose competition in tattooing in the 1970s spurred on the development of the art-form. Some of their work was almost super-realism.

10. *Use of Abstractionism, Surrealism, Impressionism, or any of the other -isms* has been very limited except in primitive cultures. In the 1930s in America some Surrealistic designs were employed and in the 1970s in New York some "psychedelic" designs were employed. The latter originated during trips on psychotropic drugs. Carol Nightengale (Washington D.C) has a style he calls "Arabesque".

11. *Stylism* has been important in many primitive cultures and might even be said to be characteristic of most American tattooing which is very uniform in nature.

12. *Choice of subject matter* has been one of originality in the early Japanese master tattooists, but in recent times stencils of already-drawn designs have been used by all but the very good tattooists such as Kazou Oguri (of Japan's Gifu City).

Some subjects have been, at one time or another temporal period in the light of prevailing mores, considered obscene. This should not affect adversely artistic evaluation, which doesn't contain all the values of a particular culture. Of course, relativity enters into the picture when an artistic creation is evaluated. As the saying goes, "beauty is in the eye of the beholder". This is particularly cogent when dealing with tattoos.

13. *Ratio of area tattooed to untattooed skin* is important unless the object has been to cover every square millimetre of available skin. The humanising effect of the untattooed areas or areas of normal skin can be effective in contrasting heavily tattooed areas. This *negative space* has been overlooked by many tattooists. If the face or hands have been tattooed, great negative social sanction will be placed on the individual so marked. Using the area of the face, in this culture and temporal era for tattooing, has been declared taboo, even though a contemporary *moko* would be a work of art. Actual facial *mokos* have been done in New Zealand by one tattooist on a few remaining Maori descendants.

14. *Shading gradations* (or gradients of chroma, hue and value) have been perfected in the Japanese and usually bungled in the American form of the art. The electric shading device didn't seem to have the subtlety of the Japanese block of graded needles, but artistic technique can make up for this deficit in the so-called Sumi-shading technique using diluted Sumi ink.

15. *Use of chiaroscuro* has been seen in most Japanese tattooing but no-where else, until recent times after 1971, or in the work of Sailor Jerry Collins of Hawaii who greatly influenced the American tattoo scene.

16, *Permanency of design* was really judged retrospectively as the tattoo matured. Some fugitive colours, such as yellow, red and vermilion faded long before carbon-based blue, before use of pigments developed, in part, by Jerry Collins. Some lines may become more blurred than others with time, which probably related to depth of tattooing and particle size and insolubility of the pigments used. Tattooing by hand lasted longer and stayed brighter than the more

superficial electric tattooing, supposedly. The chisel tattoo the Maoris were undoubtedly the most permanent of all.

17. *The pain* involved during the operation increased with the depth, the dullness of the implement and the size of the implement. This was the element of devotion to art. The largest masterpieces of the most permanence would be the most painful to acquire. The pain on the dorsal arm could be considered 1 on a scale of one — ten. Other parts of the body could be rated to 10 in the axilla (armpit).

18. *The length of time required to render a design* depended more on the proficiency of the artist and his talent than the technique.

19. *The canvas*, or the textured and stretchy surface of the skin, affected the appearance of the tattoo placed on it. The colour of the skin (black, brown or white); the texture (scarred, delicate, thin, thick or freckled) and the firmness of skeletal or bony masses beneath it made this type of canvas a difficult substrate. Tattooing was the only form of painting done on a living canvas, and possibly the first kind of painting done by primitive man, before he discovered cave walls.

20. *Limitations imposed by different techniques* seemed self-evident in that the sharp edge of a shell was certainly a more crude tool than one or two steel needles. One would have thought with the invention of the electric tattooing machine would have come the acme of the art. This has not been the case. With the electric method came speed and lowering in caste of the operator, which resulted in break-neck doodlings by persons unschooled in art. One recent American tattooist, however, has had a four-year college eduction in fine arts in the last few years. Perhaps, from his needles will originate masterpieces which will rival those of the 18th century masters Hori Chiyo and Sutherland

MacDonald. This was in 1972. Since that time other artists of professional background have entered the field and there was an International Tattoo Artists Association whose 300 plus members are trying to upgrade the profession by encouraging art-training, instilling hygienic and sterilising procedures.

Dr Lemes reports that there is no evidence to link tattooing with cancer, pointing out that laboratory animals used in cancer research have been tattooed with identification numbers for years, with no evidence of the disease. Tattooing has been linked with a number of infectious diseases transmitted through faulty hygiene, however with modern sterilisation this seldom occurs any more.

In the past diseases such as syphilis, leprosy, viral hepatitis (a danger even now), tuberculosis, tetanus and rubella have been transmitted through tattooing. The fear of spreading these diseases and AIDS has caused most tattoo studios to take elaborate precautions to ensure that their equipment is sterilised using hospital standard autoclaves, that needles and pigment containers are used once only.

As a guide if the studio is not spotless and the operator grubby, walk out and take your business elsewhere. Do not have any tattooing carried out in unsanitary premises under any condition. Backyard studios which don't measure up in the hygience stakes are not places to get a tattoo.

Some people are more sensitive to tattoo pigments than others and may develop reactions to them. Scarring can also occur but seems to be rare in the original tattooing, but is quite common when tattoos are removed, whichever method is used.

Most people suffer from a transient irritation of the skin from the punctures of a tattoo.

A few years ago laser removals were supposed to be the most effective and cause the least scarring, but in practice caused quite noticeable scarring and is seldom used today.

In the past the process involved making puncture marks and then treating the surface with a mixture of chemicals. It was effective, particularly for large tattoos but did cause extensive scarring. The tattoo can also be removed by abrasion - physically wearing away the surface of the skin to below the level of the puncture marks, but this does cause extensive and ugly scarring. The Ancient Greeks removed tattoos by treatment with special salt solutions, but it also can cause scars. Small tattooscan be removed by conventional surgery – simply cutting the image out..

It can't be stressed too highly, though - get expert help. Most tattooists, while they won't do the job themselves, know of doctors who will undertake tattoo removal, although there aren't likely to be any guarantees offered.

Bibliography

De Luca S. (Ed) — L'Asino Ela Zebra. Rome. De Luca Editore. 1985.

Fellman S. — The Japanese Tattoo. New York. Abbeville Press. 1986.

Lenars C & Lenars J. — Ritual and Seduction The Human Body As Art.
London. New English Library. 1980.

Richter S. — Tattoo. London. Quartet Books. 1985.

Rubin A. (Ed) — Marks of Civilisation Artistic Transformations of the Human Body.
Los Angeles. University of California. 1988.

Tuttle L. (Ed) — Tattoo Historian. Number 1. November, 1982.

Tuttle L. (Ed) — Tattoo Historian. Number 2. March, 1983.

Tuttle J. (Ed) — Tattoo Historian. Number 5. 1984.

Tuttle J. (Ed) — Tattoo Historian. Number 6. 1984.

Tuttle J. (Ed) — Tattoo Historian. Number 7. 1985.

Tuttle J. (Ed) — Tattoo Historian. Number 8. Fall, 1985.

Tuttle J. (Ed) — Tattoo Historian. Number 9. Spring, 1986.

Tuttle J. (Ed) — Tattoo Historian. Number 11. Spring - Summer, 1987.

Vale V & Juno A. (Eds) — Modern Primitives. San Francisco. RE/Search Publications. 1990.

Webb S. — Heavily Tattooed Men and Women. New York. McGraw-Hill. 1976.

Wright N. — Understanding Human Behavior. New York. Columbia House. 1974.

Wroblewski C. — Modern Primitives. Vienna. Verlag Christian Brandstatter. 1988.

Wroblewski C. — Skin Show The Art & Craft of Tattoo. Amsterdam. Dragon's Dream. 1981.

Wroblewski C. — Skin Shows The Art of Tattoo. London. Virgin Books. 1989.

Wroblewski C. — Skin Shows II The Art of Tattoo. London. Virgin Books. 1991.

Wroblewski C. & Cooper A. — Tattoo Art Skin Fantasies on Tattooed Women.
Vienna. Edition Christian Brandstatter. 1985

Wroblewski C. — Tattoo Pigments of Imagination.
New York. Alfred Van Der Marck Editions. 1987.

Wroblewski C. — Tattooed Women. London. Virgin Books. 1992.

Tattoo by Les Bowen
Photograph courtesy of Ozbike, Australia's Outlaw Biker Magazine

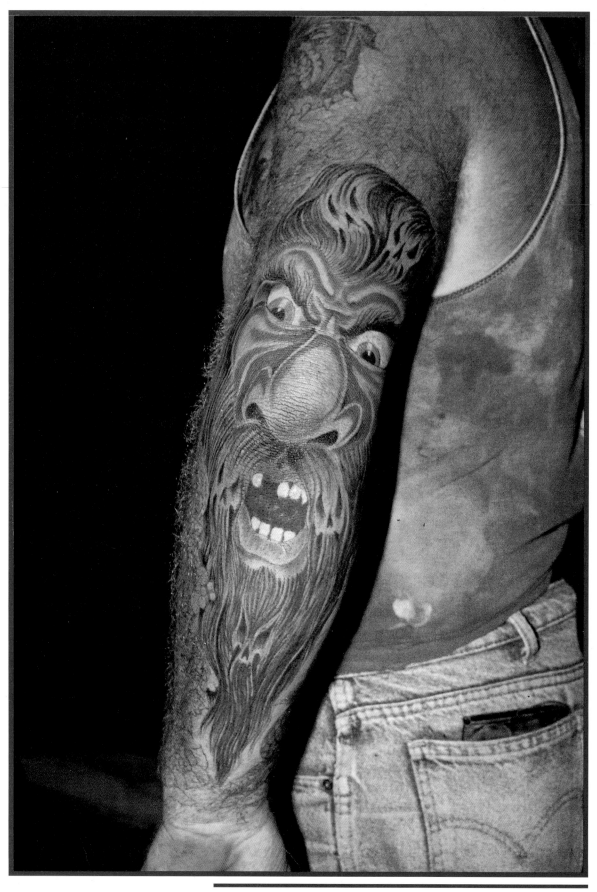

Photograph by Keith Cole
Photograph courtesy of Ozbike, Australia's Outlaw Biker Magazine